Willie Robertson was born and bred in Dundee, and started his working career at Fletcher's Diary in the city. He left school with six O Levels and then started an apprenticeship as an architectural draftsman. Two degrees and an MBA later, Willie now runs his own company providing global training in the gas and oil industries.

He still lives in Dundee with his wife and two children and is proud to call it home.

On the Milk

WILLIE ROBERTSON

First published in 2009 by
HACHETTE SCOTLAND,
an imprint of HACHETTE UK

First published in paperback in 2010
by HACHETTE SCOTLAND

1

Cataloguing in Publication Data is available from the British Library

ISBN 978 0 7553 1929 9

Typeset by Avon DataSet Ltd, Bidford-on-Avon, Warwickshire

Printed and bound in Great Britain by
Clays Ltd, St Ives plc

Hachette Scotland's policy is to use papers that are natural, renewable and
recyclable products and made from wood grown in sustainable
forests. The logging and manufacturing processes are expected to
conform to the environmental regulations of the country of origin.

HACHETTE SCOTLAND
An Hachette UK Company
338 Euston Road
London NW1 3BH

www.hachettescotland.co.uk
www.hachette.co.uk

Contents

To Carole Robertson

and

Robin Pilcher

Without them, nobody would be reading this.

Chapter One

A Journey of a Thousand Miles

A journey of a thousand miles begins with a single step.
My single step was welded to the back of a
five-ton Bedford truck.

The lorry swerved across the road and skidded to a halt, bouncing its right front wheel hard on to the pavement. Trails of steam began to rise into the cold silence from under the bonnet, and from the seven damp boys crammed together on the back. Bleary-eyed blackbirds peered down from their soggy nests on the tops of nearby tenement chimneys, and agreed to postpone the dawn chorus until this unusual occurrence had been explained.

Shortly after six in the morning, the lorry had come to a hissing stop outside a little paper shop that was just opening for the day. Nobody could remember the lorry ever deviating from the strict timetable, let alone stopping, and the lads looked apprehensively at each other and at Avril, the gaffer, sitting among the milk crates equally nonplussed.

The driver opened the cab door a fraction and called along the crack of light into the semi-darkness, 'New laddie, c'mere!'

This was only my third morning with Fletcher's Dairies and I was well aware of a 'new laddie's' place in the pecking order, so was a little apprehensive that I'd been singled out for an audience with Auld Jim Fletcher himself.

'Whit's yer name again, son?' His ancient face betrayed a lifetime of whiskies and days that began at four in the morning.

'Wullie,' I said, 'an' ye started me on Monday.'

'Oh, aye, that's richt. Wullie, be a good lad an' nip into that wee shop an' git me a bar o' skittery chocolate.'

He held out a shilling, which I knew would be more than enough to pay for any bar of chocolate, no matter how exotic, so I took the little coin from his leathery hand and nipped into the shop as ordered.

The faded sign above the shop proclaimed the

owner to be Akbar Mohammed, known to all as 'Broon Aki' because, since all his customers were milk-white in winter and bright red in the summer, his perennially dark brown skin was viewed with curiosity and even a touch of envy.

'Ane bar o' skittery chocolate, please,' I said, as if I'd been buying this product every day for the last ten years.

The little shopkeeper looked back at me with mild disinterest. 'We got every kind o' chocolate here, son,' he replied, sweeping his arm absently over a counter bursting with a rainbow of coloured wrappings, 'but we're no' stocking skittery. This is because I never heard of it.'

Back out on the pavement, I blinked up at Auld Jim in his cab. 'Broon says he disnae hae ony skittery chocolate an' he's nivir heard o' it.'

Jim looked exasperated. 'Nae bloody wonder he's nivir heard o' it. If ye eat nuthin' but foreign curries, ye'll nivir need it. Git back in there an' tell wee Broon that ye want a bar o' the black chocolate that mak's yer shite skitter if ye're blocked up.'

So, back in the shop, with as much authority as I could muster, I croaked, 'Ane bar o' the black chocolate that mak's people shite.'

The diminutive shopkeeper replied in a glorious blend of the 1930s Queen's English he'd learned at school in Calcutta and the thick Dundee dialect he'd picked up from a hundred thousand sales of fags, pies and newspapers, 'Get oot o' my shop, ye wee smart-arse. You waste my time asking for skittery chocolate when I'm getting the papers ready for my delivery laddies? If you had a proper education, you would realise that what you are looking to purchase is the chocolate laxative, which you will get from chemists, no' sweetie shops. Now tell your boss, please to get his mulk larry oot fae the front of my shop right now, for he is blocking my customers. An' dinna come back!'

The only thing that prevented Broon Aki from gaining first-hand experience of the excellent casualty facilities at Dundee Royal Infirmary, and also saved Auld Jim from enjoying yet another breakfast courtesy of the Dundee City Police holding cells, was Avril, Jim's daughter and the operations manager of the milk lorry. She pointed out to him that we were already quite a way behind schedule and the timetable of the milk round really ought to take precedence over his clogged-up digestive system: 'Ah've git sivin laddies back here doin' bugger a' fur the last fehve meenits, a' 'cos o' yer constipation. So jist git this bloody larry movin'. Now.'

Avril was right of course: the timetable was everything. Nothing but absolutely nothing could disrupt the schedule. If the wheels of the lorry ever made an unplanned stop during the delivery round, there was a full judicial inquiry, and God help the person who was to blame. So, swearing vengeance on the wee shopkeeper and half the Indian subcontinent, Jim crunched into first gear and the lorry shot off round the corner on the wrong side of the road. As it passed me standing on the pavement, I swung on to the little platform at the back as I'd been taught and took up my place beside Avril, six other milk laddies and 180 crates of milk.

'Ah've still got Auld Jim's shillin', Johnny,' I said, seeking guidance from the senior milk laddie, who happened to be standing next to me on the step. 'Ah didnae hae time tae gie it back tae him.'

'Dinna worry, Wullie – Ah'll see he gets it,' said Johnny, and took the silver coin into his 'safekeeping'. I was too new and too naïve to question the senior milk laddie's decision.

I wouldn't have been trying to buy skittery chocolate or clinging on to the back of a bouncing milk lorry in the first cold light of dawn if it hadn't been for my pal Gordon. We had become friends on our first day at secondary school and were now inseparable, so as soon as he got started on the milk with Fletcher's, Gordon began looking for a chance to get me on the lorry as well. That chance arrived only two months later, when one of the older milk laddies got a full-time job as an apprentice sign-writer and quit.

The universally accepted convention at the time was that any milk boy who jacked in his job would give sufficient notice to allow him to spend at least two weeks training his replacement and showing him the round. Unfortunately for Avril, this particular lad had been told by his new boss that several other talented young men were desperate to take advantage of such a fantastic 'oppurtuni'y' and that he would have to start on the following Monday or lose the oppurtuni'y of a lifetime. So he said he would start on Monday.

This meant that, not for the first time, Avril had to take on the role of trainer and mentor for another wide-eyed recruit. Thanks to Gordon putting in a word for me, telling Avril that I was a 'braw wee worker' and instantly available, I was granted a job interview with Auld Jim that very Friday evening, when the lorry had nearly finished collecting customers' milk money. I was really apprehensive – getting a start on the milk meant more than just taking on a part-time job, because milk laddies were a breed apart: they were real men, earning real men's wages in a real man's world. We all watched the lorry speeding through our housing estate on its way back to the depot on a Friday night, every boy secretly wishing that he was standing on the step with the rest of the guys, imagining that every girl on the street secretly wished that one of these heroes would ask her for a date. Being a milk boy carried about equal kudos with being a jet fighter pilot or a time-served welder, so on that Friday night at half past six, I donned the most grown-up outfit I had – blue denim jeans and a pale blue open-necked shirt – and headed for the interview that could change my life.

I began to suspect that Jim Fletcher hadn't read many books on interviewing techniques when my interrogation started with him sitting in his cab leaning out the window and me standing on the pavement in full view and earshot of everybody else.

Jim favoured the direct approach: 'Whit's yer name, son?'

'Wullie, Mister Fletcher. Wullie Robertson.'

'So, Wullie, Goardin telt me that ye want a start. Is that richt?'

'Oh, aye, Mister Fletcher. Ah asked Goardin tae gie me the nod when there wiz a space on the larry, so here Ah am.' I tried to say the 'here Ah am' bit with the kind of assured self-confidence that I thought all working men had to have.

'How auld are ye, Wullie?'

'Fifteen, Mister Fletcher,' trying to look as tall as I could and turning up the collar of my pale blue shirt like the teddy boys did, although I must have actually looked about twelve.

This was July 1962 and I had celebrated my fourteenth birthday only three weeks earlier: I had bent the truth a little because I figured that a more mature person would have a better chance of getting the job. I must have been right because the interview still seemed to be going pretty well.

Jim moved the discussion into the closing phase. 'Does yer faither ken ye're here lookin' fur a joab?'

That line threw me a bit because if I'd told my dad that I was trying to get a job on the milk, he would have told my mum and my glittering career as a milk boy would have terminated before it had even started. I could just hear her going on about education, and O levels, and achieving better things, and growing boys needing their sleep, until my dad gave in and banned me from ever taking a job anywhere. I'd figured that if Auld Jim actually gave me a job, it would be too late for my mum because it would be a done deal. If all else failed, I could play my trump card about having given Jim my word that I'd be there on Monday morning and say, 'How can Ah go back an' tell the lads that ma mum winna let me?'

With this in mind, I managed to retain my composure and blurt out, 'Oh, aye, Mister Fletcher, ma dad's real keen fur me tae take on some responsibility an' start makin' some money.' This was of course a downright lie.

Nevertheless, Auld Jim seemed suitably convinced that I had the makings of a reasonable employee, so the offer was made without further discussion.

'Richt, then, Wullie, ye start on Monday. Go an' sit on the back an' see Avril aboot the 'oors an' the paiye. An', Wullie?'

'Yes, Mister Fletcher?'

He smiled a big, warm smile and fifty years of graft fell from his gnarled old face. 'Ca' me Jim.'

I was overwhelmed with delight and gratitude. 'Oh, thanks, Mister— er, Ah mean Jim. Dinna worry, Ah'll no' let ye doon.'

Jim winked at me and turned back to the steering wheel, another Oliver having thanked Fagin for the privilege of joining the gang.

After my successful interview, Avril introduced me to my milk-laddie colleagues as we sat among the crates of empty bottles and sped back to the depot. Apart from Gordon, they clearly couldn't give a shit for this plonker with the turned-up collar as Avril explained to me about the ''oors an' the paiye'.

'Ye start at fehv o'clock every moarnin' except Sunday.' Gordon had already told me that turning up at five was considered late, so we should be there at ten to five at least, to help with the loading of the truck. 'Ye git one pound a week wages an' ye'll earn at least sivinteen bob in tips, mair if ye dae whit Ah tell ye. Ye start at half past six on a Sunday, so ye'll git a lang lie, an' ye collect mulk money efter yer roond on Seturdays an' Sundays, so ye'll feenish aboot twelve o'clock. Ye collect money on Friday nights between fehv an' sivin an' a'. Now, holidays, Wullie: ye git Christmas Day an' New Year's Day aff wi' paiye, an' ye git ane week aff in the summer wi' paiye. If ye want mair time aff, ye can usually hae some, as lang as ye gie me at least twa weeks' notice, but ye winna git paiyed, mind. Last thing, son: ye hae tae gie me at least ane week's notice if ye pack in yer joab, so we can git a replacemint an' ye kin show the new laddie the roond. If ye dinna gie yer week's notice, we'll keep yer last week's wages.'

I was agreeing without listening. I was gazing out at the housing estate, looking at the faces of my schoolmates standing in little groups, as we rattled past on our way back to base. I was certain that I could see a mixture of envy and respect in the eyes of every boy we passed, and convinced that every girl thought I was suddenly somewhere between Sir Lancelot and Elvis.

I arranged to see Gordon later that evening for some grown-up working men's talk about our job and then fairly flew out of the depot, filled with pride and bursting to tell somebody my good news. Since I would have to pass my grannie Robertson's house on the way home, I decided that she should be the first person to share my great tidings, so I bounced into her close and bounded up the three flights of stairs to her wee two-room flat.

As soon as she opened the door, I spilled out, 'Guess what, Grannie, Ah've got a start on Fletcher's milk.'

She looked suitably impressed, put a loving arm round my shoulders, and walked me into the hall and through to her living room, where one table, four chairs, a chest of drawers and a bed-settee were carefully arranged to maximise use of the limited available space. She sat me on one of the chairs with my back to her little TV.

'Well done, Wullie,' she said, offering me an Embassy Filter Tip, which I declined like always. She lit up her own and carried on, 'Ye're a good wee laddie an' Ah ken ye'll dae weel, but listen, son.' She leaned forward and her voice became a whisper. 'It disnae really metter whit we dae now. Them Germans, or Russians, or somebody is jist aboot tae drap an atum bomb richt on tap o' us. And, as if that's no' bad enough, we're awa tae git demolished by a huge, big haemorrhoid fae ooter space.' The little TV had clearly been keeping her well informed.

She looked worried and obviously thought that I needed to be worried as well. Her grip tightened on my wrist, so I tried to look a little bit concerned while reassuring her with, 'Dinna worry, Grannie, we'll be OK. The Russians widnae drap an atum bomb on Dundee – there's nuthin' here worth bombin'.'

She thought about that for a moment and it seemed to be making sense. 'But whit aboot the shipyaird an' the new Timex factory, though, Wullie? They're worth somethin'.'

'The shipyaird hasnae built a boat fur the last five years – even the Russians ken that – an' waars dinna get won by throwin' watches at the enemy, so we'll no' get bombed, Grannie, dinna worry.'

She began to relax, let go of my wrist and sat back in her chair, clearly relieved that a nuclear holocaust wouldn't be happening today after all. She'd obviously forgotten about my own great news, and even the giant space haemorrhoid had slipped from her mind. So I kissed her on the cheek and made for the door, where she gave me her usual little parting address: 'Now, tak' care o' yersel', stay oot o' trubble an' God bless ye.'

'Takin' care o' masel'' and 'stayin' oot o' trubble' were elementary skills I had already learned in chip-shop queues and primary-school playgrounds, and they had never presented me with much difficulty, but I always had a big problem trying to get to know the God my grannie was praying to. Even if He did exist, I never could accept that He would be able to spare any time to bless me, what with all the other stuff He must have to deal with.

'So what's in the diary for today, then, Gabriel?'

'Well, God, you've got a pretty full agenda again. You really will have to have another look at the rate at which the universe is expanding: it's accelerating at an exponential rate of linear mathematical progression of about ten to the power four, so we'll need a decision from You before the next board meeting about how we slow down the space-time continuum interface. Next, at ten thirty, You have Your weekly battle with the Prince of Darkness to try to determine, for all eternity, the ultimate struggle between the forces of good and evil. Then, after lunch, You have to deal with yet another problem from Planet Earth – You'll remember, sir, it's the fourth wee bit of water and rock orbiting round a minor star in a minor galaxy among the eight hundred squillion billion other galaxies You created during Your legendary six days of hard graft. Well, the dominant life form on this little planet is still slaughtering one another and beseeching Thee to protect their own lot, while helping them to obliterate the other lot. Then the rest of the afternoon is pretty well occupied with weighing the Book of Judgement for about seventy-four million of them who died yesterday, not including the backlog of appeals from the day before.

'But by far the most important appointment in today's diary, Your Omnipotence, is for You to arrange to keep Wullie Robertson from Dundee oot o' trubble.'

Even though I couldn't accept it for myself, I admired my grannie's unshakeable faith in her God and her saviour Jesus. In truth, I probably always envied the calm and charitable way that she dealt with the wickedness that surrounded her, saw goodness everywhere, and could explain with utter certainty what would happen to her when she passed into the 'everlasting'. Her pure, innocent belief in a God of unconditional love was the only thing that ever got near to making me question my own beliefs. Surely such goodness, articulated through people like my grannie, must eventually triumph over all the evil in the world, because love's message always wins in the end, doesn't it? Well, yes, but it sometimes depends on the messenger.

If my grannie had appeared in one of Charles Dickens's novels, her character would have provoked righteous outrage that any civilised society could allow some of its citizens to be treated so shamefully. My grannie didn't grow up as a character in a Dickensian novel, though; she lived her real life in a wealthy British city in the twentieth century, which makes the crimes that were inflicted on her and her like all the more appalling. She was born number eight in a family of fourteen children. Poor diet, slum housing and every other kind of social deprivation meant that my great-grandmother's vitamin-D reserves were non-existent, so child number eight and all subsequent siblings were born with rickets. Rickets is a condition affecting children where a vitamin-D deficiency hinders the body's ability to absorb calcium, which results in softening of the bones. Consequently, my grannie grew up with severely deformed legs and was unable to walk until she was about twelve. Nevertheless, her 'betters' sent her to work in a jute mill as a child, even though she could barely get herself to the gates, and she remained in awe of the gentry for the rest of her life

The church she committed her whole life to justified its existence by preaching, 'It may seem to some of ye that a certain preevileged few are very fortunate in this life because they have everything and ye have nothing, but ye see' – smiling face turned towards the echoing oak-beamed ceiling – 'in His infinite wisdom and mercy, He has decreed that when ye are dead, yer stations will be reversed: ye'll have milk and honey and all sorts of good things, while it'll be their turn to have nothing and be cast into the infernal pit for all eternity. Did Jesus not tell us about the rich man and the eye of the needle? So if ye just all stay in your place and do what ye're told, everything will be fine in the end.'

When you're just fourteen, though, anything that happened more than about three days ago and which didn't directly involve you is a lot less important than what's happening right now, especially if you're at the centre of it. So it was out of my grannie's close, a deep breath, a quick check at the sky for Russian bombers and off home to face my mum.

'Hi, Mum,' I shouted, as I pushed open the back door.

'Is that you Wullie?' came the predictable response and, equally predictably, 'Nae, it's King Herod, have yez ony bairns livin' here?'

'Ye're late fur yer tea, Herod. It's been in the oven fur the past half 'oor, so dinna start moanin' that it's a' dried up. Whar wiz ye, onyway? Wanderin' aboot wi' that Goardin, up tae nae good, Ah suppose?'

'Well, no, Mum, Ah wasnae wi' Goardin. Ah wiz at a job interview.'

She kept her back towards me while carefully folding the dish towel and placing it on the draining board, before slowly turning round with that blood-chilling expression that all females have learned by the age of twelve. 'Whit d'ye mean, interview? Whit kind o' a joab? Whit are ye talkin' aboot?'

I knew that this moment was the catalyst that would transform my role from child of the household to young adult, if only I had the bottle to get through the audition. I sat down at the kitchen table looking as unconcerned as I could manage, and said in turn to the ceiling, the window and the linoleum, 'It's . . . er . . . a milk laddie, Mum.'

She glared at me for a couple of seconds and her eyes never left me while she shouted through to the living room without moving an inch, 'BILL!'

My dad immediately appeared in the kitchen. 'Whit's the metter, dear? Whit's wrang?'

My two younger brothers materialised, cherub-faced, round the side of the kitchen door behind him; they smelled confrontation like great white sharks smell blood in water. Ian was nearly eleven and Gerald was eight, and they shared the bedroom next to my mum and dad. This was a major disaster for family equilibrium because the two of them were always screeching with laughter, jumping and crashing about being cowboys, or else Gerald was wailing through floods of tears after playing with his brother. Ian was constantly inventing new games and wee Gerry always enthusiastically joined in. The trouble was that Ian's games were inevitably based around similar scenarios: he was the riot policeman and Gerald was the mob, or he was the stout-hearted Scottish Jock soldier, while little Gerald represented the invading Chinese Commie hordes. It always ended up the same: Ian packed a pillowcase tightly tied up with clothes from the washing basket and belted his wee brother around the head until he started to cry. Every game concluded when law and order was none too subtly restored by Mum, and the cowboys, rioters or foreign hordes were subdued or in tears – usually both.

My younger brother's latest and most creative offering was a game called 'You Rioting Caffer'. This involved him taking on the demanding role of a South African Special Forces policeman, while Gerry accepted a vital supporting part as a rioting Zulu on the streets of Soweto. Ian must have seen some material from South Africa on the TV news and decided that this would be another legitimate excuse to beat his wee brother about the head. He managed to convince Gerry that 'rioting caffers' had spears and clubs, and offered him a little cane stick with which to defend himself against the forces of apartheid.

Of course, Gerald's wee stick was instantly swept aside, and Ian was just beginning to pummel his little brother's head and upper body when 'BILL!' rang out from the kitchen. All beatings were suspended and the caffers stopped rioting, so that wee Zulus and riot policemen alike could make a beeline for the kitchen.

Meanwhile, downstairs, Dad was handed his first clue. 'Whit's the metter is that this ane's only got himsel' a joab deliverin' mulk.'

For a fleeting moment my dad looked pleased and I thought he was going to congratulate me, but he must have realised that my mum hadn't summoned him all the way to the kitchen just to wish me well in my new career, so he quickly became all stern and fatherly. 'Well, now, Wullie. So ye've took a joab deliverin' milk, eh? Well . . . eh . . . um . . . eh . . . Whit aboot . . . ? Eh . . . um . . . ye really should hae telt yer mother an' me afore ye did this, ye ken?'

While my dad was frantically stalling for time so he could find out what the problem was, my mum's gaze fell on two little heads at the door. 'Awa', you twa, up the stairs. This is nuthin' tae dae wi' yez.'

As my brothers did as ordered and scampered up the stairs, I just made out Gerald's gleeful squeak disappearing towards the top landing, where they would of course go into SAS mode and lie quietly in a camouflaged listening post: 'Mum disnae look very pleased, Ian. Whit's Wullie done, Ian? Eh, Ian? Is Wullie goin' tae get intae big trubble, Ian?'

No doubt the listening post clearly picked up 'Oh, fur Christ's sake, Bill, tell him that we'll no' allow this. Whit aboot his O levels? An' he's far too young tae be runnin' aboot in the middle o' the night when he should be gettin' his rest. Young lads need their sleep, ye ken.'

Now that my dad had been supplied with the script, he became much more focused. 'Ye shouldae discussed this wi' me an' yer mother, Wullie, afore ye agreed onythin'. Young laddies need sleep. Ye're far too young tae be runnin' aboot in the middle o' the night when ye should be gettin' yer rest an' ye've got yer O-level exams comin' up next year, or is it the year efter?' He glanced at my mum, hoping in vain that she would supply the answer.

'Ah'm sorry, Dad,' I said. 'It a' happened so quick Ah had tae accept there an' then or he wid hae given it tae somebody else.'

My dad turned apologetically to my mum. 'Ye see how it was, dear – it a' happened so quick he had tae accept there an' then or they wid hae offered it tae somebody else.'

My mum was unmoved. 'Aye, well, he can just go back an' unaccept their fine offer. He kin tell them that he'll no' be turnin' up on Monday, because he's changed his mind.'

My dad stiffened and his voice took on an air of quiet authority. 'He'll do nuthin' o' the kind, Lizzie. He telt them that he would be there, so he'll be there. Ah'll no' hae any laddie o' mine giein' his promise, then backin' oot. If this does nuthin' else, it'll learn the lad that giein' yer word means somethin'. He gave them his word, so he'll be there wi' the rest o' them first thing on Monday moarnin'. Now, awa' an' get the tea on the table for oor new workin' man.'

I savoured the sweet mug of tea and the sausage, bacon and eggs in the kitchen with my dad, safe in the knowledge that everything had gone exactly as I had hoped.

My mum spent all Saturday morning doing her Greta Garbo impersonation around the house, sighing and looking pained so my dad and me would know that she wasn't very pleased about my career move, but she came back from her usual Saturday-afternoon trip down the town bearing a great big steak pie and a shiny new alarm clock.

'Ye'll need tae build yersel' up if ye really are goin' tae carry on wi' this nonsense, Wullie,' she snorted, thrusting the pie unceremoniously into the oven. 'An' ye'll need tae get yersel' up in the moarnin', 'cos dinna think that yer father an' me are goin' tae dae it fur ye, so this is fur you.' She smacked the alarm clock on to the table.

At her insistence, I went to bed at half past nine that

Sunday night, so I would be 'a' fresh fur startin' work'. Thoughts about what was to come that next morning filled my head and soon had me drifting into a soft, cosy world where I was leaning nonchalantly on the back of an enormous truck, being driven through massed crowds of sighing schoolgirls wearing tiny skirts and impossibly tight blouses, while huge bundles of banknotes spilled from the pockets of my trendy jeans. I lay asleep in the darkness, breathing ever more heavily and doing what fourteen-year-old boys do when dreaming about being surrounded by fawning girls who are peeling off their blouses and bras, and crawling all over them. It was warm, it was sexual, and I was just beginning to float into Paradise when the gates of Hell suddenly burst open and all of Beelzebub's demonic shrieking hordes poured into my bedroom through the ceiling.

I leaped out of bed like a startled gazelle, with thoughts of atom bombs and giant space haemorrhoids flashing through my brain. 'Holy Christ, whit the fuck's happenin'?'

The whole room echoed with a clanging cacophony of noise. My body's reflexes were on hyper red alert and were pumping pints of adrenaline into my veins, as the inside of my skull was overwhelmed with deafening ringing. I thrashed ineffectively about in the darkness for a few moments before it dawned on me that the awful deafening racket was coming out of the wee shiny alarm clock that my mum had given me. I started to fumble in the blackness, pushing every lever and button on the brass clock till I eventually managed to silence the bloody bells. I sat sweating on the edge of my bed as the cold began to pull me awake and the throbbing erection of a few sleepy moments ago metamorphosed into an earthworm.

She did this on fuckin' purpose, just 'cos Ah took the joab, I thought to myself. She must hae asked fur the loudest fuckin' alarm clock in Britain. Half the bloody street must be awake now an' she'll say it was a' down to me when everybody starts to complain tomorrow moarnin'.

I could just hear her talking to the neighbours the next day: 'Ah'm awful sorry if Wullie's alarm clock disturbed yez a'.' She would then give it her long-suffering-mother look and say things about how she tried to talk sense into me and how she reminded me about the vital importance of O levels but that I wouldn't listen to her wise words and it was a burden having a delinquent son. I could just see her Oscar-winning performance: the camera closing in on her, dressed as an Italian peasant and sobbing into a huge pot of spaghetti bolognese in a kitchen filled with seven generations of Mafia family, while she wails stuff like, 'My-a-piccolo Wullie, he-ees-a-good-a-boy. He all-a-ways respect hees-a-mamma, but he was led astray by de little-a-punks like that Goardin, who make-a-him become a mulk-a-laddie, to my eternal shame,' while the camera panned slowly out to reveal the full squalor of a little village in Sicily, or the Bronx, or Kirkton, or anywhere. I'd seen this film before, so I pulled my trendy denim shirt over my head, stuck my legs into my impractical tight denim jeans, and put on my socks and shoes. No more alarm clocks today: tomorrow morning was now, and I was a milk laddie on a mission.

I quietly closed and locked the back door so as not to waken my mum and dad, and trotted into the damp, dark morning, heading for the depot about half a mile from my house. I wasn't a third of the way to the place, though, before I realised that I had made a grave mistake in dressing to impress groupie schoolgirls when I should have been kitted out to deliver milk. It was fuckin' Baltic, and the thin rain was slowly coating my fashionable shirt in a damp, drizzly sheen, making me feel the cold all the more. I had no hat, no gloves, no vest and no warm jacket, and I was starting to lose the feeling in my fingertips. By the time I reached the depot, I looked like those horrible flickering newsreel images of troops returning from the Somme: freezing, wet, dispirited and not really wanting to fight any more Germans or deliver any more milk.

Avril took one look at me and immediately appreciated my plight, because she had seen dozens of little James Dean milk laddies before – posing like mad, looking really trendy and cool while their bollocks froze off. She sauntered over and started to explain trivia like when the truck would leave the depot and how I would then meet my fellow workers, all the while shepherding me towards the big shed where today's crates of full milk bottles were stacked, waiting to be loaded on to trucks. As soon as we were alone inside the shed, she changed into a woman and asked me if I was warm enough. I wanted to fall into her arms, curl up and whimper that I was damp and bloody freezin', and that I would love her to envelop me in her warm embrace and take me back to the time just before my mum's industrial-strength alarm clock wrenched me from the clutches of dozens of semi-naked schoolgirls. Unfortunately, as a fourteen-year-old boy in 1962, I could never, ever allow myself to admit to being cold and wanting to go home, so I did what any of us did if we found ourselves in this kind of situation: I retreated into the stories played out on the television, cinema and in *Boy's Own* magazines of the time, in which the 'wimmin fowk' mopped the brows of handsome, wounded young men and then loaded muskets for the grizzled 'real men', who wore thick rawhide jackets and had dead racoons stuck on their heads. 'Whit, me, cold, ma'am? Ho, ho, ho. Ah laugh at cold, ma'am. Ah love bein' soakin' wet, an' that last bullet jist nicked ma hert, an' even then An dinna feel nuthin'.'

Well, I sure felt somethin' – I felt fuckin' frozen and

I wanted to go home to my bed – but I didn't want Avril to think that her newest milk laddie was a whining wimp, so I came as close as I dared to admitting, in the privacy of the shed, that all was not perfect for me. 'Ah didnae think it wid be this cauld. Ah maybe shouldae put on ma big jeckett fur when we're jist standin' aboot, but Ah'll be fine once we get goin'.'

Avril said, 'OK, son, but pit this on, jist till we git goin', mind.' She bent under the shelf in the tiny wee office beside the big doors to the storage shed and pulled out a clone of the anorak that Sir Edmund Hillary had worn to conquer Everest. It was dark green, covered in toggles, pouches and pockets, and three sizes too big for me; it even had a cord round the middle so you could maintain your hourglass figure while you struggled up the North Face. It was, however, much better being a warm nerd than a frozen poser, so I pulled it over my head, strode out to where Gordon and the rest of the crew were just finishing loading up the lorry with full crates of milk, and stepped up on to the little platform at the back of the truck.

Chapter Two

Basic Training

'Give me a girl at an impressionable age and
she's mine for life.'
Miss Jean Brodie

'Gie me a laddie at an impressionable age an'
Ah'll mak' money.'
Ms Avril Fletcher

It took three to four weeks for Avril to transform a boy
from a rookie into a 'mulk laddie, second class'
(MLSC) and a further three or four months for her to
raise him to the rank of 'mulk laddie, first class'
(MLFC). All the other lads on the lorry had completed
their basic training, and two of them had even

achieved corporal's stripes. I was really anxious to become a fully skilled operative and an accepted member of the team, so threw myself and my oversized anorak into learning mode with a vengeance.

Basic training started with practicalities and etiquette – what would now be called risk assessment and safety training. Today, it would take three months working with six experts from some expensive consultancy practice, eight separate inspections from six different 'cooncil' departments and a twenty-week review of the Company Quality Manual by the Health and Safety Executive before a single laddie was anywhere near a milk bottle. Avril gave me everything I needed to know in fifteen minutes.

This was no five-miles-an-hour electric milk float; this was a five-ton Bedford truck like the army had, except that it was a flatbed version with a narrow standing platform welded on the back, and above the standing step was a tubular metal grab rail, called a holding (huddin') rail, at an average fourteen-year-old's waist height.

The lorry carried nearly two hundred crates of milk, each holding forty-eight glass pint bottles, and it covered the round at up to forty-five miles an hour with seven milk laddies hanging on the back. It was potentially a very dangerous place to be, so the first morning's training was all about safety, lesson one being 'how to stand on the back of the lorry without endangering your own life or anyone else's'. The men who crewed the whaling ships that hunted in the freezing seas of the North Atlantic endlessly drummed the mantra 'One hand for the ship and one hand for yourself' into the heads of their inexperienced young shipmates, and it was exactly the same on our little vessel. Keeping at least one hand on the holding rail at all times was the primary rule.

Avril was a good teacher – after all, she'd had more than a hundred pupils to practise her skills on over the years – so her lessons were no-nonsense, tell-it-like-it-is and straight to the point. 'Right, Wullie. Aye, keep baith yer hands on the huddin' rail at a' times. Keep ane o' yer hands on the huddin' rail if ye're loadin' or unloadin' bottles, an' nivir, ivir hae nane o' yer hands on the rail, an' Ah'll tell ye fur how. Ye see, the larry micht go ower a wee bump or roond a coarner an' ye'll loss yer balance an' fa' aff the back an' split yer heid an' kill yersel', or ye micht grab the laddie next tae ye an' pull him aff as weel, or worst o' a', ye micht grab on tae a mulk crate an' pull it aff the larry an' smash a' the mulk.'

Fair enough, I thought, not wanting to blot my copybook either by getting killed or smashing a whole crate of milk on my very first day. So my debut as a fully fledged apprentice milk laddie consisted of very obviously keeping both my hands on the huddin' rail while Avril gave me the next lesson: 'How to get on and off on a moving milk lorry'.

The lorry very seldom actually came to a standstill during the round, so it was vital that every laddie knew how to get on and off the back step safely while the vehicle was moving. This was much more difficult than it sounds, because we were loaded down with full pint bottles of milk getting off the lorry and carrying up to sixteen empty glass bottles in wire carriers getting back on. All the other lads could carry up to three full bottles or four empty ones in each hand, so Avril showed me how to place three bottles between my fingers so that they pressed against each other and could be carried in one of my hands. She then demonstrated how to insert my thumb and three fingers into the necks of four empties so that they could also be transported using only one hand.

Of course, the point of this part of the training was simply to help Avril maximise the efficiency of her little group of workers by trying to shave every second off the time it took for each lad to complete his delivery and get back on the truck. The more efficient each boy became, the more customers could be fitted in. The game therefore was to get off the lorry without getting hurt or without it having to stop, deposit the correct number of pint bottles in front of every door on that little section of your round, pick up the empty bottles that had been left for collection, and then get back to the pavement and on to the lorry as quickly as possible.

The methods of getting off and on varied slightly, according to the number of doors you were working and the number of bottles you were carrying, but the basic technique was simple, dangerous and very effective.

Avril explained all this to me with detached clarity. 'Now, Wullie, if ye've only got ane or twa doors tae deliver an' ye're only cerryin' twa or three bottles or a single cerrier, ye'll hae a free hand.'

She went on to describe how this was the easiest drill of all because you simply took the bottles or the wire carrier in one hand, let go of the rail with the other hand and stepped backwards off the platform. You landed on the road at jogging speed and sprinted to your first delivery. Meanwhile, Auld Jim carried on, dropping off another four laddies in the next street, or a couple of lads in the next close or whatever, before coming round again for you.

When you came back on to the pavement, you put all the empties you had collected in your hand or in the carrier and prepared the other hand for pick-up. As the lorry approached, again at jogging speed, the other lads moved over to leave one end of the platform free as it passed close to the kerb on whichever side of the road you were standing. 'Ye jist grab the huddin' rail as it passes ye an' gie a wee jump up on tae the step.' A combination of your leap and the lorry's momentum was supposed to swing you on to the step, where you then clunked your empties into the crate that Avril had waiting for you. Most of the time it worked.

Non-milk-deliverers might well think that this specialised training would have limited application in the wide world beyond the round, but they'd be wrong. It had benefits that far exceeded the simple delivery of milk. One Saturday morning, Gordon and me were heading into town and rounded the end of our road just in time to see the bus moving away from the stop and driving towards us. By the time it reached us, it was going almost as fast as we could run, but neither of us hesitated for a second. In those days, all double-decker buses had a rear open platform on the pavement side, with a vertical steel pole on the outer edge. Gordon and me instinctively stood a couple of yards apart, and as the bus went past, I grabbed the pole and flicked myself on to the platform, followed half a second later by Gordon. We didn't think anything of it; it was just like the many times when Auld Jim was dreaming a whisky-flavoured dream and whipped his lorry to the gallop, forgetting that one of his laddies was waiting at the kerbside to be picked up.

The bus conductor didn't seem to share our relaxed attitude, though, and his shaking fingers scrabbled frantically at the bell button, dinging for all he was worth. The bus came to an abrupt stop and the white-faced conductor pounced on Gordon and me. 'Whit in the name o' God wiz that? Are yez tryin' tae kill yersel's?'

We just stood on the platform and looked sheepish, but when the driver appeared at the platform, the dynamics shifted. This guy was seriously hard. He had the look of someone who was no stranger to a pub fight, and the tattoos on his arms reached down to just above his wrists, so when he told us, 'Get tae fuck aff ma bus,' we instantly obliged.

We stood at the bus-stop feeling cold and foolish, waiting for the next one. After a couple of minutes' silence, Gordon whispered, 'Bet Ah can git on mair gently than you, Wullie.'

I turned and saw him mimicking a refined nineteenth-century lady stepping delicately into a horse-drawn carriage. I started to giggle and responded with a reasonably bad impression of an arthritic ninety-year-old getting on to a bus. By the time our transport arrived, we were giggling so hard that we had to hold each other up. The bus stopped and Gordon put the toe of his right foot demurely on the step and held out a limp left hand towards the conductor for assistance. I almost couldn't look at him for laughing as I clutched for the metal pole and made a great show of slowly pulling myself eighteen inches up on to the step. This conductor wasn't amused either, and I think we were a heartbeat from 'gettin' tae fuck' off our second bus in a row.

The wire carriers we were equipped with held up to eight pints. Laddies could take a carrier in both hands, which gave each of us the capacity to deliver sixteen pints of milk at every run. That was a combined potential of 112 pints of milk on the move at any one time. Of course, the problem was, with a carrier in each hand, you would have to break rule number one: 'Nivir, ivir hae nane o' yer hands on the rail.' So the drill was that Avril squatted on the back of the lorry, filled a couple of carriers, and slid them in front of the lad doing the next section of the round, who would be standing on the rear platform with his back to the road. The lorry slowed to trotting pace, while a comrade on one side gripped the shoulder of the lad's shirt or jacket, allowing the boy to let go of the rail and take a carrier in each hand. As the dropping-off point was reached, the person holding him on to the lorry let go and the laddie stepped backwards off the platform and hit the ground running. It was a technique that had been perfected over many years, and I never saw an accident involving anybody getting off the lorry, but standing there on the wee step with both my white-knuckled hands holding the rail, I could see that Avril was beginning to detect the first signs of a severe dose of lack of moral fibre in her latest recruit.

'OK wi' that, Wullie?'

'Nae problem, Avril,' I said, trying to look as cool and nonchalant as my galloping pulse rate would allow, while my eyes involuntarily flicked between the step, the rail and the road surface speeding past under the truck.

'Right, then, let's git on tae how tae git back on the larry wi' a cerrier in each hand.'

The idea here was that Jim slowed to a fast walking pace while the lad getting back on trotted behind the truck and offered both his carriers up to his mates. Their job was to take the carriers out of the lad's hands, which would allow him to make a simple little hop on to the platform and grab the rail. Dead simple in theory, but occasionally a wee bit more problematic in practice, as my hands, knees and elbows found to their cost several times as my career progressed.

I wasn't to know that then, of course, and I'd been watching the other lads gliding smoothly on and off the lorry since we'd left the depot, so when Avril asked me if I was 'Awright wi' that?', I managed to shrug my shoulders and drawl, 'Nae problems fur me, Avril. Nuthin' in it, really, is there?'

I was anxious to appear eager to progress, so I asked if we could move on to learning my round, but Avril's years of experience were way ahead of my youthful bravado. 'Ah think ye should practise gettin' aff an' on for a wee while afore we move tae the next bit. Whit d'ye say?'

'Oh, well,' I said, trying to look disappointed while

hiding my relief, 'if ye really think so. Ah'll dae whitever ye think's best.'

So for most of the rest of the morning, I had to practise getting on and off the moving truck – first with the thumb of one hand hooked into my belt, then with an empty wire carrier in one hand and finally with a full carrier in each hand. By midway through the first morning, after hundreds of left- and right-hand combinations of stepping on and off the lorry and miles of bumping along keeping both my hands on the 'huddin' rail', I was ready for solo flight.

If only I'd come home after my first morning and seen an advert on our little black-and-white TV that said, 'Have you had an accident at work lately? We at Slightest Pretext specialise in cases of employer negligence, and remember, no win, no fee,' then my financial situation might have been very different during my teens. The advert would probably have highlighted the case of Tam or Joe or some other laddie who would appear onscreen looking suitably serious and well rehearsed, saying something like, 'There was I, goin' about my normal duties as a milk delivery person when the larry suddenly swerved an' I lost my grip on the huddin' rail. I fell aff the back an' severely skinned my arse, an' Slightest Pretext got me twenty-five pounds an' ten shillings.' But they didn't have opportunities like that back then – you just rubbed your skinned arse and got on with it, so I had to turn up for work at the huddin' rail the next day.

One morning, standing on the step between my runs, I suddenly thought that Count Dracula would have made a great milk laddie. His preference for nocturnal activity would be a huge asset in the winter as he raced between the pre-fabs in total darkness with a carrier in each hand and his black cloak streaming behind him.

They could even have made a film about it. *Son of Dracula the Milk Laddie* might have been a smash hit. Fleeting glimpses of a badly skinned arse recovering its pink smoothness in the blink of an eye, or scraped Romanian knees healing themselves in three celluloid frames would have been perfect for a 1960s B-movie. I could just see the audience peering through the fog of cigarette smoke at the Prince of Darkness running up closes in the pitch dark of a Scottish November morning.

Despite Avril's excellent training programme, things were a wee bit different in practice. It was usually quite dark at the start of the round and we were all pretty tired by the end, so either darkness or fatigue sometimes caused a laddie to concentrate more on getting his carriers handed over than on getting himself back on the step. When this happened, he would catch a toe on the edge of the platform or even miss it completely with his leading leg, resulting in quite a few heavy landings on the road. As if that wasn't enough for us to worry about, Jim almost always took off far too fast once a laddie was back aboard, which was even more dangerous, because the boy could miss the grab rail and end up going backwards as the truck accelerated, which would cause much more serious injury than the split lips, skinned knees, bashed heads and bruised elbows that came from missing the step.

Getting safely back on the mother ship is a lot more difficult than getting safely off, as milk laddies and the guys who fly jet fighters from the deck of the USS *Nimitz* know equally well. When you're leaving a milk lorry or a nuclear-powered aircraft carrier, you just relax, lean back and let it happen, but getting back on needs concentration, judgement and skill, especially when it's dark and you're tired, which is why US Navy fighter pilots would probably make superb milk laddies. 'Homerun One, Homerun One, you are four feet downrange, height five foot two and approaching at six miles an hour.'

'Roger that, Full Cream. Now have visual contact with the huddin' rail. Am making my final approach.'

Thirty years after I'd received all this training, students studying for master's degrees in business administration at Harvard Business School would learn that Japanese corporations were pioneering the radical philosophies of Just-in-Time production and Total Quality Management, which would revolutionise the way the whole world did business. These 'JIT' and

'TQM' disciples wandered the corridors of their huge corporate headquarters in Detroit or Houston quoting Japanese war manuals and saying things like, 'Right first time, on time, every time,' to impress the impressionable. They truly believed that the West would suffer economic collapse if we didn't embrace these revolutionary concepts that Japanese industry had invented. But they were all misled by their management gurus and university professors, because, as every milk boy knows, JIT and TQM were already being practised by guys like Auld Jim Fletcher in 1962. The Just-in-Time philosophy was expressed as 'God help ye if ye're no' standin' at the kerb when the larry comes back tae get ye' and the Total Quality Management ethos was articulated as 'If ye're no' pleased, ye can piss aff.'

Before I could ever hope to understand these advanced management theories, though, I had to complete the rest of my basic training.

'If there's an amergincy o' ony kind, pick an empty oot o' a crate an' start bangin' it on the flair o' the larry. Huld it roond the middle so it winna smash in yer hand an' bash the bottom on the deck. Jim'll hear the signal an' stop right away. Got that? Good. Now, if ye ivir see anithir lad, or even me, pickin' up a bottle an' giein' the signal, you imeejitly pick oot a bottle an' dae the same. Dinna stop tae ask whit's wrang. Jist keep thumpin' yer bottle till the larry stops.'

Ever anxious to play the diligent pupil, I nodded my understanding. 'Ah'll dae that if ivir Ah hae tae, Avril, bit how d'ye ken if it's a proper emergency?'

'Aw, that's good thinkin', son.' She seemed pleased with my foresight. 'Amergincies is things like when somebody fa's aff the back or misses the step gettin' on, or even if the crates slide an' trap yer fingers in between. But my faither's gettin' aulder now an' he whiles forgets the roond, so we sometimes hae tae gie the signal tae remind him tae slow doon an' let a laddie git aff or come back on. Are ye fine wi' that, Wullie?'

It seemed clear enough to me. 'Aye, Avril.'

Now that I understood the emergency procedures and was deemed to be reasonably safe getting off and on the lorry while laden down with bottles, the next phase of Avril's training programme dealt with collecting milk money. I had naïvely thought that this would be a pretty simple part of the job: I would knock on the door and say, 'Milk money, please'; the householder would pay me; I'd check off the amount against a list of what was owed, put the money in the wee leather bag; and, after doing this routine with a few customers, I would take the bag back to the truck and give the money to Avril. I was very soon to find out just how far from reality this was. Over the next twenty minutes, Avril opened my eyes to the art of milk-money collection while I stood on the little back step of the truck like a doe-eyed convent novice in Sir Edmund's anorak.

'There's three perts tae collectin', Wullie. First, ye've tae git the money fae the anes that paiye ye; second, ye've tae deal wi' them that say they canna paiye ye or hae some excuse or moan or other; and third, ye've tae get yersel' as much tips as ye kin.'

Avril was more aware of what makes people tick than the best behavioural psychologists in Britain, and she focused this vast expertise towards helping her dad's small business to prosper and helping her laddies to maximise their tips. After all, the more tips we got, the lower the wages she needed to offer, thus helping her dad's business to survive. In twenty minutes, she had downloaded a PhD's worth of information and I could hardly keep up with the flow.

'Now, Wullie, first thing ye dae is find oot their name, 'cos fowk love hearin' their ain name. Ye'll git that aff the list at the start, but ye'll learn them a' soon enough. Next, ye chap on the door an' as soon as it's opened, ye gie a big smile an' say, "Hello, Missus Whitever. Ah'm yer new mulk laddie an' Ah've been deliverin' yer mulk fur the last week. Ah'm here to collect yer mulk money." The anes that always paiye ye'll smile back, say hello and hand ye the money. Now, this is very important, Wullie: if the customer gies ye the right money an' nuthin' else, look as if ye're tryin' no' tae let on that ye're disappointed – look at the money, pit it in the bag, gie her a wee saft smile and leave.'

I was holding the wee leather book Avril had given me with the lists of customers and amounts they owed, and trying to concentrate on her wise advice, but my mind kept wandering to the fact that the book felt vaguely spongy and smelled of stale milk.

Avril was in full flow now. 'If the customer gies ye too much an' needs cheenge, always coont the money back so the last coin ye put in her hand is the ane ye want as yer tip. Let's say, fur example, she gits ane pint a day except Sundays – that's six pints a week, which is four bob. Suppose she hands ye two half-croons, so she's gae ye fehv bob an' she's waitin' fur a shillin' cheenge: nivir gie her a shillin' back. Ye slowly coont oot twa sixpenny bits, an' if she thanks ye an' gies ye nuthin' fur yersel', look a wee bit disappointed, but dinna say nuthin', 'cos ye'll ken she's no' a tanner tipper. The next time, gie her the cheenge in ane sixpence and twa thrupennies, makin' sure the last coin ye gie her is a thrupenny bit. If she nods an' gies ye nuthin', look a wee bit disappointed, but dinna say nuthin', 'cos ye'll ken she's no' a thrupenny tipper either. The next time, gie her the cheenge o' ane sixpence, ane thrupenny an' three pennies, makin' sure the last coin ye gie her is a penny. Tak' yer time gettin' the last penny. Rake aboot in the bag fur a while an' sometimes they'll get fed up an' tell ye to keep it.

But if she stands there till ye're done, thanks ye fur the cheenge, and still gies ye nuthin', look a lot disappointed, but dinna say nuthin'.'

Johnny whispered in my ear, 'An' hae a wee smile tae yersel', 'cos ye'll ken she's goin' tae be unlucky next week – a big tom cat'll probaraly smash a bottle on her step one moarnin' tryin' tae get tae the mulk. Shame, really – nae mulk in the moarnin' an' gless an' mulk a'place ower her step, eh?'

I was starting to feel nauseous as the little book felt ever more revolting between my fingers, and the smell of old milk-soaked leather and paper increasingly filled my nostrils.

Avril continued on a roll, 'The next anes, Wullie, are the moaners an' them that say they canna paiye ye or hae some excuse. The moaners tell ye they didnae get ony bottles last Tuesday, or they swear they telt us they wiz goin' tae be awa' fur the weekend an' we still delivered them mulk. Sometimes it's the trooth, but it's usually shite. When ye git them stories, jist say, "I'll hae tae ask aboot this," an' come straight back tae me on the larry. Ah'll tell ye if they're chancers or honest fowk, an' if they're chancin' it, Ah'll come back tae the door wi' ye an' sort it oot. Dinna worry, lad, ye'll soon git tae ken them that are always affy unforchinit wi' the missed deliveries. Then there's the anes that canna paiye, an' they're the best tippers o' the lot. They'll ask if they can paiye double next week, or paiye half this

43

week an' mak' the rest up next week. They're at least admittin' that they owe the money, an' they usually git it paiyed when she has a win on the bingo or he gits some overtime or comes up on the horses, but they a' paiye up in the end. When they do paiye up, though, it's cake an' cookie time, 'cos they gie a huge tip tae mak' thirsel's feel better. Are ye clear wi' that now, Wullie?'

I wasn't at all clear – it was information overload – and I suspected that tomorrow Avril would school me in how to get myself two cups of tea and a slice of dumplin' from every house I collected. For the moment, though, I nodded obligingly and said I understood completely.

'That's grand, Wullie. Ye'll get yer chance tae try it oot on Friday, but fur just now, we'll look at yer roond. The moarnin' an' fur the next few moarnin's, Ah'll hae tae come wi' ye tae show ye yer deliveries, 'cos that wee sleekit shite Judy left withoot workin' his notice.'

For the rest of the shift, the other lads scurried around delivering huge quantities of milk with seamless military precision, while I stood on the platform in my big damp anorak, trying desperately to remember the scores of houses and doorways that Avril identified as part of my round as we sped past. At last the lorry, now stacked with crates of empty bottles, reversed back in front of the big shed in the depot. The lads got off the back and started to make their way towards the gate, home, breakfast, then school. It was just after eight, and Gordon and me swaggered down the road as if we'd just finished a fourteen-hour shift in a South Wales coal mine; we were working men, you see, and working men are allowed to swagger.

The next morning, I was prepared for the alarm clock from hell, so I arrived less traumatised, in good time and properly dressed in my own warm clothes, so I wouldn't have to trouble Sir Edmund again for the loan of his anorak. For the next three hours, I tried to cram my head with the information that Avril reeled off as she ran me through my round, pointing at doorsteps. Her memory was remarkable, mind-boggling: she was like these guys on the telly who answer questions on any subject put to them by the studio audience. 'Who won the Cup in 1932? What was the score? What was the line-up of each team? Who were the ball boys?' and the 'Great Memoro, the Finest Mind in England' would flawlessly rattle off the information. That was Avril: 'Wallace gits ane pint a day, dead simple. Neish gits four pints a day: she's got six bairns. McCleod an' Robb git ane pint, but Robb gits twa on a Seturday. Auld Mrs Nichol gits a pint every second day, an' Selway gits ane pint an' ane cert.'

I had to ask Gordon what a 'cert' was and he informed me that it was a bottle with a gold top, which meant that somebody somewhere had certified something. This went on all morning till my head was exploding with names and numbers and routes up closes and shortcuts across backyards.

'Ye'll learn it a' soon enough, son, dinna worry yersel'. Now fur yer breakfast, Wullie: between aboot half past six tae sivin o'clock, ye lift a roll oot o' any bag that the roll laddies huv left on a step. Tak' it oot gently an' put the bag back exactly whar it wiz. Jist the ane roll, mind, an' nivir the same doorstep twice in a row. We a' club in fur a jar o' jam aboot once a week, so we've a' got somethin' tae put on oor roll. Eat it while ye've git twa meenits waitin' fur the other laddies tae get back tae the larry.'

It took a couple of seconds for this information to sink in. I could never have questioned Avril's instructions or the accepted practice on the larry, and I certainly didn't have any pangs of conscience about nicking a quarter of some poor householder's legitimate breakfast, but it appeared to me in my naïvety that it wouldn't have needed Sherlock and Watson to deduce what was going on, so my one and only concern was for my own safety: I might get caught.

I could visualise my crimes being exposed before my mum and dad and everybody who knew me as they sat in the 'one-and-nine' seats of the Odeon cinema, staring at the screen through a fog of cigarette smoke while engrossed in the latest Scottish production of *The Case of the Vanishing Roll.*

'I have deduced Watson that it wiz that wee mulk laddie Robertson that done it.'

'You astound me, Holmes. How could ye possibly work that oot?'

'It wiz elimen'ary, Doctor. I perceived flour marks on the huddin' rail an' roll crumbs on the flair o' the larry. Pass me ower anithir wee pinch o' that opium.'

'See you, Holmes – ye're amaizin'.'

'But they're bound tae ken it's us that's daein' it, Avril – there's naebody else aboot.'

Avril gave a patient little smile. 'Listen, Wullie. 'Coorse they ken it's us, but provin' it's a different thing. We tak' eight rolls oot o' the thoosands they deliver every moarnin', an' we nivir tak' fae the same door twice. Naebody's goin' tae set up a police stakeoot fur a roll. Besides, the roll laddies steal oor mulk.'

Chapter Three

The Crew

If only Geoffrey Chaucer had lived in Kirkton:
what a tale he could have told.

The lorry operated with a crew of nine: Jim Fletcher, Avril and seven assorted milk laddies. The milk-delivery lads were as diverse a collection of humanity as Chaucer's pilgrims on their way to Canterbury, and their tales were no less interesting. The only difference was that Chaucer's travelling companions were on a late-fourteenth-century pilgrimage to a holy shrine in Canterbury, whereas us pilgrims were on a mid-twentieth-century journey through Dundee to get more tips. Same thing, really – each group being driven by a desire to reach its own Nirvana.

Auld Jim was born old, and grew steadily older in the caress of his beloved whisky. His ilk worked huge Clydesdale carthorses, wore thick leather belts and braces, flat bonnets and white shirts with no collar, and rolled up their sleeves above bulging biceps. Jim's happiest memories were probably of heaving great churns full of milk off the back of the cart, watched by a small knot of rosy-cheeked girls that one day included Mary Steadman, his future wife. Jim and Mary had two children, James and Avril. Jim must have thought that his world was complete and he had secured the Fletcher milk dynasty for ever, but along came the world in the overtaking lane and, try as he might, Jim couldn't keep up.

The fickle hand of Fate could easily have flicked embryonic Avril into some womb within a wealthy Norfolk family instead of sending her to be the daughter of Mary and Jim Fletcher in a family of Dundee milk and cream suppliers. Just in case the stork got a bit mixed up in its delivery, though, clever old Fate had equipped this particular embryo with innate qualities that could be applied equally in either life. She was a handsome woman with fine blond hair, an athletic body and clear, mischievous eyes, and she would have looked as striking gliding around in a glittering silk gown at the Hunt Ball as she did in stained overalls loading milk crates on to the truck. Her greatest talent was her ability to control and motivate a pack. It wouldn't have mattered if it was a pack of foxhounds out on the hunt or a pack of milk laddies out on the make; Avril had extraordinary organisational skills, which came to the fore whenever a task needed to be accomplished. The Norfolk Hunt's loss was Dundee's gain, as Avril Fletcher applied her leadership abilities to inspiring and cajoling the little pack that made a profit for her and her dad.

She started by getting to know the personal tale of each of her own wee pilgrims.

Johnny Bonnar's Tale

Johnny was the dominant alpha male on the truck and, at almost sixteen, was at least a year older than any other laddie in the squad, and more than a year and a half older than me. He'd been on the milk for ever and knew all the rounds, the dodges, the best tippers and the scams he needed to make him the best earner by a mile. He really thought he was the dog's knob, but our problem was that we did too, so all of us with our 'short back and sides' haircuts deferred to him and hung on his every word like he was a Japanese sensei. Johnny didn't just stand on the back step of the truck; he struck a pose with his groin thrust forward and his Brylcreemed hair fully exposed to the rush of the slipstream, so he would look wild and unruly and rebellious.

He didn't speak words like everybody else; he let them slide out of the corner of his mouth as if he was Elvis's twin brother, kidnapped from the Presley family home in infancy and spirited away to a council estate in Dundee, so he always spoke as though he was trying to integrate his natural Dixie drawl with the guttural Dundonian growl: 'Have yez heard the King lost a tooth an' nearly swallied it? Hey, man, that wid hae been like somethin' oot o' *Jailhoose Rock*. Real bad news, man.' We were all mightily impressed when he did his Elvis bit, whistling every 's' like Cliff Richard, and liberally sprinkling 'man' and 'daddy-oh' over every sentence he uttered.

We thought he was great, and agreed between ourselves that the only reason he lowered himself to being a milk laddie was that he was saving up to buy a motorbike. He often brought in the shiny catalogues and pointed out the bike he was going to get, a Triumph Tiger. Even the names 'Triumph' and 'Tiger' fitted perfectly with his image and his status, but it wouldn't have mattered if the bike had been called a 'Vanquished Rabbit'; we still thought Johnny was everything we wanted to be: cool, tough, wild and masculine. We never could have foreseen that he and his ilk would soon be washed away by a tidal wave of young teenagers who didn't care for leather or motorbikes or grease, kids who didn't give a monkey's if the King swallowed either his tooth or his motorbike and would have cheerfully used his sacred blue suede shoes to clean the toilet, as long as the splashes didn't stain their Cuban-heeled Beatle boots.

Johnny was completely obsessed by anything sexual and spent most of his time talking about girls and tits and wanking and shagging. Every second morning, we would hear a graphic story about some young girl he had been with the night before, and how he had fondled her bare breasts while she 'wanked him till he shot off'. Of course, we believed all this crap and Johnny's sexual exploits took on legendary proportions. We were all pubescent young males and certainly no strangers to the joys of masturbation, but Johnny did it better, longer, more often and more spectacularly than all the rest of us put together, and we were in awe of this stud on the back of our truck. As a result of his obsession with his penis, Johnny went around in an almost permanent state of partial erection, which he called his 'semi', and his right hand was constantly in the pocket of his jeans, performing a dexterous juggling act somewhere between adjusting and fondling.

He may have been a sexual obsessive, but he was a class act when it came to getting tips, because he knew exactly what he was trying to do when he knocked on the door of the many young, and not so young, housewives to collect their money. He was actually quite a good-looking young lad, with enough style and youthful charm to momentarily divert the attentions of a few of his housewife customers from the daily grind of cleaning the sink and cooking mince. He knew it, and played it for all it was worth. Because of his semi, he always had a huge bulge in the front of his jeans, so he would knock on the door and stand a pace or two back off the step, looking dead cool, with his legs slightly apart to show off his semi to its maximum advantage while still allowing him to appear as innocent as Adam before his daft bird ate the apple.

'Milk money, please, Missus McKenzie,' he would say in his Cliff Richard voice, while furtively glancing at the woman's tits or her legs as if he couldn't help himself but didn't want to be seen doing it. The sight of a handsome young boy with a big bulge in his trousers trying hard to control his inflamed youthful passions persuaded four or five of the more neglected housewives into giving Johnny a ridiculous tip because he made them feel attractive and sexy for a couple of minutes once a week. Of course, the overwhelming majority of women he collected from must have found it difficult to suppress laughter at his Casanova impersonation, but they still gave him a good tip for providing a bit of light relief from the hoovering.

Deep down, I knew there was never a serious possibility that any of the women who enjoyed a few moments' diversion from their boring routine would actually do anything about this charade, but I still gazed at Johnny doing his doorstep act and fantasised about the few women who looked as if they just might go for it. What would it actually be like to be invited inside by one of them to have my every adolescent sexual dream made reality? How would it start? What would she do? How would I know what I was supposed to do? So it wasn't only Johnny who had biker gangs of hormones screaming around his body with nowhere to go: all the rest of us could be just as easily aroused by peeking down the cleavage of a woman, even one as mature as thirty, when she bent to count the money into our hand, or by getting a flash of thigh from some young mother as her kid pulled at the front of her dressing gown. Consequently, we often ended up with a bit of a semi ourselves.

Although Johnny's strategy generally paid off and he made more tips than any of us, the price of his success was that he often came back on to the lorry in a severely distressed state. 'Did yez see the tits on that?' he would breathlessly moan, subconsciously readjusting his semi. Or, 'Did yez see the way she knelt doon when she drapped her purse? She did that on purpose so I could see up her skirt, yez ken. She's desperate fur it.' It would have been interesting to see what would have happened if one of those women had taken Johnny up on his implied offer and asked him into her house. Mrs McKenzie would have smashed his bravado on the step of her pre-fab as thoroughly as her cousin Lorelei smashed sailors on the rocks of the Rhine.

Steven Devlin's Tale

At fourteen, Steven Devlin was still trying to master joined-up writing and struggling with the mysteries of long division, although every now and again he dutifully turned up at the recently opened Kirkton High Secondary School to be part of the national education experiment that was going on at the time. Steevie attended what were known as remedial classes, where kids who would now be recognised as having special needs were instructed in how best to cope with being failures. Well-meaning people tried to show Steevie how to divide 136 by 18, while other, equally devoted teachers told him about nouns and pronouns because they really believed that this would be useful to him someday. Trying to teach this stuff to Steevie was as pointless as trying to get one of Crazy Horse's Sioux braves to perform differential calculus, but if the word 'intelligence' means the ability to respond and adapt to prevailing conditions and get the best out of what's available in your environment, then Steven Devlin was by far the most intelligent among us.

Steevie hated arithmetic, which he called 'hard workie oots' because he didn't really care if Michael was three inches shorter than Mary, who was two inches taller than Mark, and he didn't see any point in it all, anyway. But if you wanted to know what your winnings would be if you bet two shillings on a three-way accumulator at Royal Ascot and gave him the odds, Steevie would tell you in an instant. The problem was that the arithmetic curriculum in the 1960s had nothing to do with bets on horses, or Steevie, or the world of any of the people he knew. It was all about grocers who bought huge chests of tea at a given price and then sold the contents in tiny wee bags at several different prices. The point of this obsession with grocers buying and selling tea was to teach pupils the basic rules of arithmetic, while explaining the relationship between the various components of the British imperial system of weights, measures and currency. So hundredweights, stones, ounces, bushels, pecks, roods, feet, inches, quarts, furlongs, pounds, shillings, pence and even guineas figured large in every exam question.

Steevie could never understand why people needed him to answer, or even read, these stupid questions. They always seemed to be woven around a plonker who borrowed money from a bank, inevitably at a huge rate of compound interest, so he could buy seventy-four roods of land and plant fifteen furlongs of some crop or other, which he would sell at nine guineas per peck once it was harvested. 'Did he make a profit, and if so, what was his remaining debt to the bank at the end of year two?' the exam question would inevitably ask. 'Who gives a fuck?' was the equally predictable response from all those in Britain who were in the equivalent of Steevie's class and trying to ascertain the market value of a roll of stolen school-dinner tickets.

He enjoyed the occasional cigarette, and by the time he was fourteen, he was on a daily intake of at least twelve Woodbines. He only needed to buy a packet of ten every day, though, because he had a wee trick up his sleeve: although the flimsy little cardboard packet he bought contained only ten flimsy little fags, Steevie also carried a wee tin box where he kept what he called his 'nippers'. He never stubbed out a cigarette or threw it away; he nipped off the lit end between his thumb and forefinger and put the half-inch stub in his tin, where he also kept a supply of cigarette papers and occasionally some of the larger discarded fag ends that he had found during the day. Once he had gathered enough tobacco to roll a cigarette, he took a paper from his nipper tin and did the business, reducing his need to buy new cigarettes every time. Whenever he lit one of these foul roll-ups on the back of the lorry, Avril would start to sing, to the tune of 'Who Were You With Last Night?', 'Woodbine's a braw wee fag,' while the rest of us followed with the backing chant 'Gie us a light! Gie us a light! Gie us a light!' I often wonder why

Imperial Tobacco didn't contact Steevie and the rest of us to do a national advertising campaign.

Steevie's dad wasn't all that big, but he was as strong as an ox, the colour of mahogany and the spitting image of Popeye. He was a brickie's labourer and was earning pretty good money, given that the whole of Britain was one big building site at the time. Mr Devlin liked his pints of McEwan's and nips of Bell's even more than Steevie liked his Woodbine, so most of his hard-earned cash went over the bar of the Silver Birch. This local hostelry probably looked really trendy in the architect's sketches given to the planning department, with the building surrounded by little trees and couples sipping white wine in the rock garden. In reality, it was a featureless, graffiti-covered, flat-roofed concrete monstrosity, stuck right in the middle of a big housing estate on a desolate square of patchy grass and dog shit. The Silver Birch had even less welcoming rustic charm than Colditz, but it was every bit as functional, because once men were inside, it was very difficult for them to get out. Steevie's dad chaired the 'Let's Not Bother Trying to Escape' Committee, and wallowed in the warmth of captivity with the rest of his dart-playing mates.

We were walking home about half past seven on a cold, dark Friday night in the middle of December after collecting milk money. A big Christmas tree covered in fairy lights illuminated the graffiti around the entrance to the Silver Birch. Several decorated wee plastic trees had also started to appear in the windows of some of the houses in the streets round about. Steevie's house was two or three hundred yards up one of these streets, and as we got closer, we began to see that the Devlin family's window display almost rivalled the Birch's contribution.

Their Christmas tree was huge, at least six foot six, and it completely dominated the whole window space and half the living room. It was covered in every kind of garish festive adornment imaginable, while the glare from the billion little red, green, blue and yellow lights hanging off every branch made the Blackpool illuminations look like a couple of forty-watt bulbs.

'Holy shit, Steevie, that's totally magic,' says Gordon, choking back his laughter and surprise. 'Where the fuck did yez get a tree like that?'

Steevie beamed with pride. 'Best in the street by a mile, eh, boys? Better than ony other hoose in the whole toon, probarly.' He was clearly revelling in our astonishment and admiration of his family's yuletide window decoration, and he savoured the feeling for a few moments before delivering the knockout punch he'd been saving since we first saw his tree. 'It didnae cost us nuthin',' he proudly proclaimed.

The brief glance that Gordon and me exchanged confirmed that we were both thinking along the lines of 'OK, Steevie, so yer tree's bloody great, but dinna start wi' the bullshit here.'

I half smiled at Gordon and said, 'How d'ye mean, it didnae cost yez nuthin', Steevie?' like you would say to a child who had told you an obvious lie. 'How could a great big tree like that no' cost yez nuthin'?'

'Peter and Tommy got it oot the crem.' He beamed. 'They went up tae the crem twa nights ago an' cut it doon. There's loads in there, ye ken. Yez could get ane each fur yersel's, if ye're quick.'

'So whit ye're tellin' us, Steevie, is that yer twa big brothers chopped doon a fir tree in the grounds o' the crematorium, an' that's yer Christmas tree?'

'That's the ticket,' he fairly crowed, openly relishing the admiration now. 'I bet ye're sorry that ye didnae think o' that yersel's.'

Gordon was first to break the spell. 'D'ye ken this, Steevie, we'd nivir hae thought o' that.'

Russell Malcolm's Tale

Russell and his mum lived in a four-storey block in one of the less desirable parts of Kirkton. Since Kirkton was one of the less desirable parts of Dundee, and Dundee itself was one of the less desirable parts of Britain at the time, Russell, his younger sister and his mum didn't often throw dinner parties for the jet set.

Nowadays, Russell's mum would be described as coming from a 'blended single-parent family unit', but in 1962, she was 'awa' fae her man'. It didn't really matter that Russell's dad was the one who had pissed off over the horizon; it was his mum who bore the stigma, while she did her best to bring up her kids on her own. She did a magnificent job, and Russell always had football boots and went on school trips like the rest of us, but we were young and self-centred enough not to appreciate what an effort every day must have been for her. She was only in her late thirties and quite a good-looking woman, but she had one of these tired faces that you see on people who are carrying a whole heap of worries and haven't had a holiday since God knows when, and we all thought of her as 'just Russell's mum'. The trouble was that the few eligible men she came into contact with also thought of her as 'just Russell's mum'. She worked on the assembly line at the Timex factory on the new industrial estate during the week, where I'm sure she derived immense personal fulfilment looking through a big magnifying glass as she put together her daily quota of watches. Then, every Saturday, she spent another eight stimulating hours slicing bacon and selling tins of beans in the Co-op store up the road.

Her son, Russell, wasn't just clever, he was special. He was outstanding in every academic department, although his real abilities were most apparent when he was dealing with mathematical or scientific subjects. However, after we left the primary school, his schoolmates, including me, would never again see this in a formal context because, when we moved to secondary school, none of us could hope to be in the same classroom as Russell ever again.

At primary, when we actually did share a class with him, it was obvious to all that Russell was different. He loved arithmetic even more than Steevie hated it, and could tell you how many pounds of tea the grocer had to sell while the rest of us were only halfway through reading the question. The reason he didn't spend all his school life getting beaten up in the toilets for daring not to be mediocre was that he never flaunted his intellectual prowess. When the teacher asked if anybody knew the answer, Russell just sat there. Everybody knew that he knew, especially the teacher, but Russell would simply look down at his book hoping somebody else would pipe up.

He also had a razor-sharp sense of humour. The ability to make others laugh was probably his best defence at primary, so when we started at Kirkton High School and met some of the pocket Al Capones from the other schools that filtered into our glittering new comprehensive, Russell was well established as a good guy with too many mates to make him one of the easy targets that bullies can spot at fifty paces.

By the time he reached Kirkton High, he was known

to all as Si, a name he'd earned at primary school as a play on the Simple Simon character of nursery-rhyme fame. Like Simple Simon, he always seemed to be both sublimely happy and a bit preoccupied without any obvious reason – traits that gifted people and daft people share in equal measure. The rest of us didn't know what the hell was inside his head half the time.

Perversely, the only person on our truck who was even remotely on the same wavelength as Si was Steevie, the very one who couldn't have been further away from him by any recognised method of measuring intellect. Si and Steevie related really well because they provided the yin to the other's yang, with each of them representing extreme opposites of what defines human intelligence. When we were about to be moved from primary school to secondary, we were given two types of test so we could be streamed according to our abilities and potential. One was a traditional examination to test our academic ability, and the other was a test to determine our 'Intelligence Quotient' or IQ. Si probably scored 101 per cent in the formal examination and was off the upper limits of the scale in the IQ test, whereas Steevie must have got about 12 per cent in the exam and didn't even register on the IQ scale.

Nevertheless, they shared a unique bond when their worlds overlapped, and each drew inspiration from the other. Every now and again, Si's enthusiasm and his supercharged brain would overcome his need not to seem different from the rest and he would blurt out some new stuff he'd been reading as if we should all be as excited as him. It was during one of those lapses that I realised that Si and Steevie were very much on the same plane, and suddenly saw that they were the only two on the truck who had a meeting of minds. Si had mentioned that he had been reading about some great new exploratory work in molecular science that was being done at the University of Somewhere.

'What stuff is that, Si?' Gordon foolishly asked, and Si couldn't restrain himself from trying to explain about molecules and atoms and all that shit.

Everybody else turned off right away, but Steevie perked up, 'Atums! That's whit they fill bombs wi' now, eh, Si?'

Si looked nonplussed, which was very unusual for him. 'Whit d'ye mean, Steevie?'

'Well, they fill big bombs full wi' atums an' then they drap them an' the atums burst oot an' kill a'body, eh?'

Even though for Steevie, atoms were like solid ball bearings packed into a big iron shell, Si realised that he understood the concept that nuclear weapons were designed around a sudden unbelievable release of energy. 'That's it,' says Si. 'But they're usin' atoms fur good things as well.' I'm sure Steevie thought that this meant 'atums' were also useful for filling holes in the road.

Si didn't work on the milk so he could buy more things for himself like the rest of us; he *needed* the job to help support his mum and little sister. Every night after school, groups of sweaty young boys and hormonal young girls met and mingled at the front gate, making smart-arse comments and generally acting stupid before sauntering off in groups of twos and threes in the general direction of home. Not Si: as soon as the bell rang, he trotted straight out of the gate and headed for a primary school about half a mile away to pick up his wee sister, walk her back to their house, then get the table set and the tea on for his mum, ready for when she came home from work.

Russell was the most intellectually gifted person I've ever met, and one of the most considerate. One pitch-black morning in early November, we all enjoyed an extra hour in bed because the clocks had been switched to British Winter Time.

'This puttin' the clocks back's fuckin' great,' Steevie announced, as he leaped merrily on to the step to begin the round. 'How do we no' put back the clock every week?'

After five awkward seconds as each of us tried to find a way to explain to Steevie just how preposterous this notion was, Si said, 'Good thought, Steevie. It's a wonder nane o' the politishuns hae realised that.'

*

Robert Findlay's Tale

Everybody called Robert Findlay 'Fat Boab' after the character in the Oor Wullie stories. Why? Because his name was Bob and he was fat. When Boab reached the final year of primary school, his doting mother was giving him five shillings a week pocket money, which was at least four or five times what the rest of us got, and he spent the lot on chips, crisps, toffee, ice lollies and chocolate. He lived on a diet of puddin' suppers and fudge bars, and you could guarantee that Boab always had enough confectionery secreted about his person to keep a chocolate-worshipping commune supplied for a year.

God knows why he ever wanted to become a milk laddie. It could have been something to do with his family's Calvinist work ethic, or maybe his mum had begun to realise that five bob a week was putting a bit of a strain on the family budget. In any event, Auld Jim must have been in the embrace of a particularly fine malt the day he started Boab. The wee fat lad already had enough money to keep him in all the pie suppers and chocolate he could consume, which were the only things that seemed to interest him, and everybody could see that the effort of running up and down tenement stairs with carriers full of milk was putting increasing strain on his round little body. Anytime he had a long run to make or a delivery on the top floor, he would arrive back on the step pissing sweat and gasping for oxygen through his fat, red face.

When we had swimming at school, Fat Boab looked like a narwhal. His skin was white to the point of being translucent, and he just sort of bobbed along, displacing gallons of water into the drainage channels around the sides of the pool with every ponderous movement of a round arm or chubby leg. At the beginning, some of our classmates squatted in giggling knots, while a skinny little comedian called Peter Dunbar, known to all as 'Horace', entertained everyone by firing an imaginary harpoon into Boab's blubbery carcass. This soon stopped after Boab came out of the pool at the end of one of Horace's particularly hilarious sessions, transformed himself from a whale into an angry rhino, and smashed the spindly little harpooner's face into the white tiled wall of the communal showers. Captain Ahab's sniggering crew instantly deserted, stepped gingerly over the blood and soapy water making its way towards the plughole, and lined up to enlist in the ranks of the Friends of Moby Dick Society. Hands up all those who thought that 'fat' means 'placid'.

Fat Boab's family were right into Presbyterianism. They were typical of the honest, hard-working families who supplied thousands of Scottish missionaries to spread God's Word, guilt and smallpox among the world's unfortunate heathens. They had no blemish of bigotry or sectarianism in their make-up; it's just that they couldn't understand why some people didn't see everything the way they did, so they didn't feel the need to parade along city streets wearing silly hats and sashes like waiters in Latvian cafés; the Findlays preferred to do their marching in church halls. Every Friday night, Boab, his father and his big brother donned dark trousers, dark jackets and dazzling-white webbing belts so they could march around the Kirkton Village Church Hall in step to approved marching tunes bashed out by a woman who was nearly as old as her piano. They had everything they needed: heavily embossed flags attached to brass-topped flagstaffs proclaimed that they were the Fourth-Fifth Boys' Brigade, while the four lads behind the flag-carriers, who blasted out occasional ear-splitting calls on gleaming brass bugles, added to the military pomp of the spectacle.

The marchers had white belts round their waists and across their chests, and the officers and the lucky ones carrying the flags got white gloves as well. Best of all, they had four gloriously decorated drums played by four gloriously decorated young drummers who could make even wooden legs tap in time to the thumping beat. Drums are great if you want to do a bit of strutting.

Back at the Findlay household, Boab's mum, who was even fatter than him, was perpetually engaged in grilling bacon and frying chips. She was one of those people whose glass was always half empty because she thought that joy and sunshine and warmth were somehow sinful, so she had spent a lifetime amassing a huge database of negative phrases for every occasion. If we said it was a 'smashin' day', she would reply, 'Aye, weel, that's as mibbie, but it'll be cauld winter soon enough,' and she always described life as 'a sair fecht' (a painful fight). Like many of her generation, she followed every reference to events in the future with the words 'if we're spared'. So you got things like 'Next Seturday, if we're spared, Robert will be goin' tae see his auntie Mary in Glasgow.' My grannie and most of her cronies used to mouth the same words when talking about things yet to happen, but whereas she was confident to entrust her future to God's tender mercy, Mrs Findlay managed to make it sound as if she'd be downright disappointed if any of us actually did get spared.

I'd known Boab from way back at primary, and we used to go together to the children's matinée performance at the local cinema on Saturday mornings. I soon got to know not to say anything cheerful to Mrs Findlay when I called for her chubby son, because she would always have a suitably dark response in her repertoire. One morning, I told her that it was my wee brother's birthday and her reply was, 'Aye, weel, Wullie, ane year mair o' his life an' ane year less.' I was quite chilled.

These matinée performances took place in cinemas throughout Britain, and kids were encouraged to think of themselves as being members of an exclusive club named after their own particular cinema, although the format was exactly the same in every picture house in the land. We all sang a song about 'coming along on Saturday morning, greeting everybody with a smile'. Boab didn't have time to greet anybody with a smile, because by the time we got to the end of his road, he was on his second Mars bar. After the 'Saturday-morning' song, there followed a couple of hours of old cartoons and black-and-white movies where cowboys chased each other around remarkably similar-looking hills, or Flash Gordon pursued Ming the Merciless across the galaxy in a silver-painted washing-up-liquid bottle with a sparkler firework sticking out of the end. After a couple of hours of this, they played 'God Save the Queen' as hundreds of children fell over sticky seats and sticky each other to get to the toilet or back out to the street, while Fat Boab stood solemnly to attention, alone amid the mayhem, till the last notes of the national anthem had died away.

However, the same passionate loyalty Bob extended to his monarch, he also gave to his friends. You couldn't ask for a more sincere, honest, faithful friend than Fat Boab.

*

John Murray's Tale

Remember when you were young and first went exploring or camping with your mates and somebody always fell in the river or got stung by wasps or broke his wrist? Well, that was John Murray. John's relationship with Lady Luck was a bit one-sided: he wanted to be her best friend, and she totally ignored him. So if you're ever playing roulette in a casino in Vegas and you see John Murray betting on red, put everything you have on black, because you can be dead certain that Lady Luck didn't come in with John.

By the time we moved to secondary school, each of us had spent countless hours waiting for John to fix his puncture, scrape the dog shit off his shoe or rub his legs with dock leaves after he had fallen into a ditch full of nettles. If John had been the pilot of a Flying Fortress bomber during the Second World War, he would have had the words 'Nearly made it' stencilled on the side of his aircraft above drawings of three playing cards: two unrelated picture cards and a two. Just under the cockpit would have been four or five representations of bombs that had failed to detonate and an RAF roundel depicting the Spitfire they had shot down by mistake.

John could probably have got through life quite well just being unlucky, but he carried another cross: he had a master's degree in gullibility. He was the most simple, honest, glaikit person I have ever known, the kind of lad who awakens protective maternal instincts in older women and evil instincts in schoolboys. Groups of twisted little bastards revelled in feeding John all kinds of nonsense and watching his reactions, and giggling little packs would watch from the sidelines as some bigger lad spun John a preposterous yarn that he would invariably swallow. Even so, I couldn't help liking John, because although he believed in Santa and the Tooth Fairy, he also believed that everybody was innately good, and that the guy with the white cowboy hat would always win in the end. Taking the piss out of John was a bit like kicking a cripple: it got boring after a while, 'cos neither of them would kick back.

They say bad things come in threes and for John this was so very true. The Great Croupier in the sky dealt him his third low card when he formed him 'in his own image', because if man really is formed in God's image, then John was a living contradiction of Michelangelo's vision on the Sistine Chapel ceiling. If Michelangelo had met John Murray before he started his epic commission, he would have painted God as a wee, skinny, spotty creature, reaching out to Adam with an arm like a little white pipe-cleaner. He was the model for the 'before' guy in a body-building advert.

The final irony was that John had a resounding bass voice. Even at fourteen he could have recorded 'Old

Man River' and made a few bob; unfortunately, Johnny Cash beat him to it with a song called 'Big Bad John', which was a top-ten hit at the time. 'Big Bad John' was about this guy who worked in a coal mine in Pennsylvania and was a real hard man; he was built like the proverbial brick shithouse and had fists made out of things like iron and steel. Johnny Cash was all black leather and macho, and had an even deeper and more gravelly voice than our own dear John, so both the singer and the song encapsulated everything that a 'real' man should aspire to, especially if you were fourteen, didn't work in a mine, had fists made out of soft, pale flesh and bone, and lived in Dundee. John Murray's mind was too fertile a pasture for us to resist planting little acorns about the relative talents of himself and Johnny Cash.

Making comparisons between the two of them was ludicrous, of course, but it was just too good an opportunity for us to miss, so we tried to convince John that he was a star waiting to be discovered. 'Ye sound jist like him, John – it's uncanny. See if you wiz tae record a sang on yer big brother's tape recorder an' send it tae EMI or somebody, ye'd mak' a forchin.'

A tiny flame of scepticism still flickered. 'Ach, c'mon, lads, ye're takin' the piss – ye ken Ah could nivir be a real pop star.'

We were aghast. ''Coorse ye could, John. Ye sound the very same as Johnny Cash, an' we've even wrote a sang fur ye tae record in the same style as he diz so ye kin send it tae a record company.'

The little flame lighting John's path to reality was finally extinguished. 'Well, we'll see. Ah'm no' promisin' nuthin', mind, but Ah might jist gie it a go tae keep yez happy. Whit's the sang, onyway?'

Johnny handed him a piece of paper. 'Ye see, we wrote it in the same style as "Big Bad John", but we changed the words a wee bit tae mak' it mair suited tae yersel' an' tae show that ye're musically adaptable. Whit d'ye think?'

In a cruel parody of Johnny Cash's 'Big Bad John', the first verse of Fletcher's milk laddies' song went:

Every morning at the depot you could see him arrive,
He stands four foot ten and weighs 'bout 105;
Kinda narrow at the shoulder and narrower at the hip,
And everybody knew you didn't give no tip to
Wee John . . . Wee Good John.

'Ye bastards. I kent yez wiz takin' the piss.'

So of course from then on we all called him 'Wee Good John', or just 'Wee Good'.

*

Gordon McKinley's Tale

Keith McKinley set off for India in his late twenties, just after the Second World War had ended and the incredibly lucrative Dundee jute trade had entered its 'maturity' phase. The whole city and its many millionaires depended almost exclusively on the revenue from selling the rough utilitarian cloth that covered pioneers' wagons, provided sandbags for both sides in the American Civil War, and formed a backing for almost every square yard of carpet in the world. By 1946, however, Indian businessmen were starting to get a bit pissed off with having to send their crops of jute to a remote town in Scotland to be spun and woven into cloth, and began to have the effrontery to believe that they could do that bit themselves. It didn't take a genius to figure out that India was soon going to build thousands of weaving and spinning mills and Dundee's jute barons needed to be part of the act if their empires were to survive; after all, even the most desperate of Dundee weavers couldn't be counted on to accept two rupees a month. So young Mr McKinley and his Higher National Certificate from Dundee Technical College were dispatched to Lahore to get their feet under the table.

Within a year of his arrival, Keith had met and married a stunningly beautiful local girl, and before his second year there was out, she had given birth to their son, Gordon. Eighteen months later, Gordon was joined by his sister, Fiona, and for the next five years, brother and sister chased lizards among the magnolias and listened to their servants' romantic tales about beautiful Indian princesses and heroic princes who took on the form of Bengal tigers to defeat wicked demons. All good things must come to an end, however, and when Gordon was nine, he and Fiona were sent to live with their grannie in the little village of Kirkton on the outskirts of Dundee, 'fur the sake o' their educashun'. It must have been a real culture shock for the two children, coming from a land of softness and colour and light to a place that was hard and grey and pitch dark for half the year.

Every summer, Gordon and Fiona were flown out to visit their parents for four weeks during the school holidays. While the rest of Gordon and Fiona's classmates went to pick raspberries for fourpence a pound in the fields around Dundee or splashed about in the freezing waters of the North Sea off Carnoustie Beach, the two children watched polo matches under a scorching sun, sitting next to two strangers who were once their mother and father. So by the time I met Gordon when we started secondary school, he spoke and acted like an orphan. On the few occasions when he mentioned his mum or dad, it was like he was talking about casual acquaintances or just people he'd met on his last trip.

Despite her most valiant efforts, Grannie McKinley was unable to exert even nominal control over her grandson. Gordon had had nine years of servants' pandering to his every whim, so he didn't take well to a strange old woman telling him what he could or couldn't do. It only took a couple of years for him to exert his will completely over the tiny pensioner, and by the time I met him at secondary school, he was doing more or less whatever he liked. He treated his grannie like the Japanese treated their emperor: she had unlimited notional authority but no actual power.

I was hugely envious of his freedom and he was hugely envious of my home life, so we came to an unspoken *quid pro quo* by which Gordon treated my mum and dad as his surrogate family and I helped him fire steel-tipped arrows into the walls of his grannie's house from a powerful bow his dad had brought back from India. Four or five times a week, Gordon and me ate our tea in the kitchen round at my house before we went on secret missions in the woods to the north of Kirkton, after stopping off at his grannie's house to arm ourselves with two huge kukri knives from his father's collection.

It seemed to me like Gordon and Fiona lived in a museum. All sorts of weird Indian and Oriental stuff was scattered around or hanging from the walls, and I always felt really uncomfortable surrounded by rugs that had heads, and pictures of women with six arms. Creepiest of all, though, were a two-foot-long stuffed crocodile-type creature whose shiny glass eyes stared at me from the top of an intricately carved black wood table, and a wastepaper bin that was the bottom nine inches of an elephant's leg. Gordon's house felt dark, threatening and sinister, and I could never get out into the air quickly enough: you never could tell when his mum and dad might ship over a wee zombie.

I think that's one of the reasons why Gordon enjoyed being at my place so much. Everything in our house was light, bright and ultra 'contemporary', either Formica or teak-effect laminate, and there wasn't a single amputated elephant's foot to be seen. My dad had just bought a luxury laminated teak-effect radio-gram with impossibly long, spindly brass legs that took pride of place in the living room and demonstrated our sophisticated appreciation of modern interior design. Gordon truly loved sitting with us like a real family member, while my dad twiddled knobs and flicked switches till the diamond-tipped needle finally filled the room with Frank Sinatra's latest big hit.

All my other mates lived in exactly the same houses, with exactly the same sunburst clock on the wall and exactly the same dad saying, 'Now that's real music, son – no' like that screamin' Elvist o' yours. Ye canna understand a bloody word that boy's sayin'. He jist shouts an' grunts. Aye, but oor Frank Sina'ra can sing, though, eh? Listen tae that melidy, Goardin.' Gordon didn't live in a house with a sunburst clock on the wall, and his dad was seven thousand miles away, sipping a gin-and-tonic on the veranda and listening to Frank Sinatra on an old gramophone. So while me and my brothers tried hard to ignore our dad and his music, Gordon would say things like, 'Right enough, Mr Robertson. He huz got a good voice.'

Gordon was my best friend in all the world, but at times like that I wished we'd had an elephant's-leg wastebin for me to honk into.

Avril Fletcher's Tale

Just two months after I joined the crew of the milk lorry, Avril turned forty. She made no effort to disguise the fact; indeed, she seemed quite proud of her achievement, and even gave each of us a little bit of her birthday cake, which we washed down with some of yesterday's undelivered milk.

For fourteen-year-old kids, forty is 'old' – even older than my own mum and dad, who were well into their dotage in their late thirties – but Avril was different somehow. She easily looked ten years younger than her true age, with light, almost platinum-blond hair that fell delicately over the side of her face when she hoisted the crates of empty bottles to the front of the truck.

I suppose she could best be described as 'striking', in an Arian, perfect-womanhood sort of way, but of course none of us would admit to thinking in these terms about the person who was our gaffer, our paymaster, our favourite auntie, our friend, our soulmate and the only woman who ever spoke to us the way we spoke to each other. It somehow felt sinful to look at Avril any other way.

But the result of a million years of evolution can't be managed on demand, so when she stretched back to lift an empty crate, or bent forward in her summer T-shirt, or pushed the next batch of full crates towards the huddin' rail with her long legs, I knew I wasn't the only boy who was trying hard to concentrate on Spitfires, or maths classes, or liver and onions, or bloody anything except what was in front of me. Although what was in front of me was pretty special.

Avril was slim, athletic, graceful and supremely feminine. Her skin was pure white and flawless; in fact, she reminded me of a tablet bar produced at the time by a company called Lee's, appropriately named Milkmaid Bar. It too was white, smooth, delicate and blemish-free, and I'm sure Avril's skin would have contained as much vanilla and sugar as the bar itself. However, her career choice as gaffer of a milk truck had forced her to hone her skills in disguising her attractiveness and femininity, so she dressed like an elderly pig farmer, gave orders like a sergeant major with an ingrowing toenail, and swore like the best of the inmates at Kirkton High.

She did have a sort of love life, though. Avril was married to Sandy Alexander, but still operated under her maiden name of Fletcher. She probably did this because her husband's full name was, unbelievably, Alexander Alexander. God knows what his loving parents were thinking about when they named him; they probably thought that Sandy Alexander was a fitting tribute to the clan memory or something – either that or they were just plain daft. Of course, everybody referred to him as 'Double Ecks'. Naturally, Avril didn't want to be known as 'Avril Double Ecks', so she never wore any rings ''cos they micht catch on the cerriers', and she never brought Double Ecks to the depot.

Avril had no children, which is not surprising when you work from four till eleven every morning with two days off a year, and your husband works nine to five every weekday. We did get to meet her only 'bairn' every day, and he had a higher IQ than the whole crew of the lorry put together – minus Si, of course. Every morning, a sleek and deadly athlete called Sabre greeted each milk laddie arriving at the gates of the depot. He was a superb example of a young, strong, very large short-haired German shepherd, and his dark brown eyes positively sparkled with vitality. He welcomed you at the gate with his sweet, killer canine smile, sniffed you, and then almost dismissively nodded you towards the truck. But if a stranger arrived at the gates and Sabre didn't recognise their scent, the fur on the back of his neck stood up, he smiled even more sweetly and nudged this new guest towards Avril, then sat beside her waiting for instructions.

It was obvious that the dog was completely devoted to his mistress, and if she had said, 'Kill him, boy,' you would have been shredded in moments. I never found out if Avril took Sabre home to the cosy Double Ecks homestead in the evening, or if he slept in the depot shed under the milk crates, because Avril and Sabre were there every morning before any of us arrived, and they were still there when the last milk laddie had left.

Avril Fletcher must have resigned herself to being heiress to a milk-delivery business and gaffer on a milk lorry by the age of about twenty. What a waste.

Chapter Four

Finding Gordon

'Can yer mum speak Inglish as good as us?'

On 24 August 1960, two years before I started the milk round, the most modern comprehensive school in Scotland had thrown open its newly varnished doors to its first intake of wide-eyed pupils, together with a couple of city councillors who wanted their photographs in the evening paper and a local MP who saw this as a way of getting himself on the national news. The facility was brand new, and the local papers had been trumpeting for months about how fortunate Dundee was to have a flagship comprehensive school, complete with sports fields, a swimming pool and metal-fabrication workshops that rivalled the best manufacturing factories in the world. Even the national broadsheets occasionally displayed photographs of scaffolding and tower cranes to make sure we remained suitably excited. Seventy million cubic yards of concrete later, a fine morning sun warmed the three hundred or so kids arriving at Kirkton High School to begin their secondary-school education.

Everybody milled around in little groups on the big chequered piazza in front of the main entrance where we had been told to assemble, looking for faces that they knew and gazing in awe at the fabric of the new school. It was straight out of a brochure for Butlins, with walls made of glass squares and pastel-coloured plastic panels, partly obscured by newly planted trees and huge pots full of exotic plants. Even though the whole place smelled of paint, and joiners were still hanging doors, while bulldozers busily transformed piles of gravel into tennis courts, the place was already something special.

Bear in mind that this was a school with no tradition, no uniform, no heroic Latin motto, heraldic badge or school colours, so we must have looked like a right motley crew with everybody dressed as they or their mum thought appropriate for the occasion. Most of the boys, including me, wore grey flannel shorts, a white open-neck shirt and sensible shoes, while others wore an assortment of leather jackets and denim jeans above their big brother's pointed winklepickers. Some had even walked straight out from the pages of books about Neanderthal man's journey through the Middle Palaeolithic period, and they wandered around in packs of three or four sporting torn T-shirts, murderous grins and battered sandshoes. The majority of the girls wore a grey or blue skirt with a white blouse and white ankle socks, but some looked like twelve-year-old apprentice hookers with tight little skirts and lacquered hair, trying to attract the attention of the Neanderthals.

By about half past nine, the teachers had managed to get everybody more or less standing in rows and had begun to shepherd the babbling throng into the main assembly hall, which was even more impressive than the glass and plastic vista outside. It was massive, designed as an auditorium to hold at least eight hundred people, with a vast domed ceiling painted matt black and a raised stage along the whole length of one end. At the back of the hall, the biggest concertina room-divider in Britain separated the assembly hall from the dinner hall, and it was designed to be pulled open to form one vast arena capable of seating all fifteen hundred pupils that the school would eventually cater for. I'd never seen anything like it. Everything was pine or stainless steel or glass, and the scale of the structure was overwhelming. There were rows of box spotlights on silver tracks suspended from the ceiling, above ranks of gleaming wooden chairs that nobody had ever sat in, laid out on a polished hardwood floor that no one had ever walked on. Gradually, the shepherds funnelled the staring, open-mouthed rabble into the lines of chairs until, after about twenty minutes, the whole lot of us were seated facing the stage.

I felt like a frightened, confused child sitting in my polished chair trying to deal with this enormous assault on my senses and emotions, while trying even harder to look as if I wasn't fazed. Some of the boys looked so grown-up, dressed like little teddy boys, laughing and joking with their mates, while directly in front of me a tall, skinny youth in a dark lounge suit, crisp white shirt and a regimental-style tie rubbed shoulders with a wee scuff in his Findus the Fisherman outfit: wellies, dark jeans and a thick woollen rollneck jersey. I didn't know either of the two kids I was sitting between, which made it even worse; we had all tried to stay beside people that we knew, but the chair-allocation lottery soon split everybody up. On my left was a large girl with a spotty complexion who was wearing her complete primary-school uniform including blazer with badge, while on my right was a lad who was a bit too tanned to have just got back from a fortnight in a caravan in Arbroath. I smiled a wee nervous smile at the lad and got a wee nervous smile back; well, at least I'd made contact with an equally lost soul.

Throughout history, those with power have included

spectacle and pageantry among their toolkit for keeping others in their place. The architects of the first ever morning assembly at Kirkton High School had learned this lesson well, because trivial details like lack of tradition or identity weren't going to stop them from laying pomp and circumstance on thick. So the stage was filled with men and women in black cloaks with coloured hoods down the back who were making a big effort to look as if Black Rod could interrupt them at any moment. Some of the cloaks even had fur round the neck and down the hood, which made the wearers look even more sinister, like giant crows that had just eaten a cat, and the spectacle was crowned by a wee round woman in a child-sized black cloak, sitting at stage left in front of an adult-sized grand piano.

Curtains on the opposite side from the piano suddenly opened and two guys moved on to the stage. One of them had on a dark grey suit, and even before I had spotted his dog collar, the ten-degree sideways tilt of his head and his great big vacant grin confirmed that he was a member of the clergy. The other lad was much more imposing, though, and his scarlet cloak fairly swished across the stage as he half bowed to his seated colleagues before ushering his reverence into a chair and floating up to the microphone. He introduced himself as the rector, which was a term I'd never heard, and then proceeded to tell us for the next fifteen minutes how lucky we were. 'You should all feel proud to be attending the first, most modern, fully comprehensive school in Scotland.' Finally, he told us that he would work with us if we would work with him, and that we were all part of a team; he'd obviously been on courses.

After his address, he introduced the Reverend Clive Greenhill of the dark grey suit as our school chaplain, another term I'd never heard; I'd only been at this school for half an hour and I'd already learned two useful new things. Clive carried his ten-degree head up to the microphone and began his address. Right from the opening words, me and the brown lad in the next seat had a fit of the repressed giggles, because Clive was obviously born and bred in Fife, but wanted everybody to think he came from Kensington. Clive and his affected accent were funny, but not that funny. It was more that I felt overwhelmed by the whole event and needed to grasp at anything that provided a release from all this nervous tension. I'm sure that the brown lad felt exactly the same, because the more we looked at each other, the more we giggled and drew comfort in each other's nervousness and apprehension.

'Thees ees a seengular honour fur one tae be called upon tae be chaplain tae such a seat of learning as this beautiful new school. Ah see this masel' as the start of a fascinating journey – a peelgreemage if you will – for us all.' The lad next to me was bent forward and silently shaking, half of his left fist stuck in his mouth. 'So let us all join together tae celebrate our new school by seenging "To Be a Peelgreem".'

The wee round wummin on the piano belted out the last line of the chorus to give everybody the key, and then we all started. The howling masses soon got into full swing: 'Hooo-oo woood troooo vaa-a-lurr seeeee let him kum hithirrr.'

Me and the brown lad were almost crying with suppressed laughter now and I ventured, 'Whit's this daft sang aboot?'

'Fuck knows, pal; it's somethin' tae dae wi' peelgreems an' hobgoblins an' fowil feends.'

After biting my lip for a couple of lines, I couldn't resist asking, 'Hey, mate, whit's a hobgoblin, onyway?'

'Oh, everybody kens that, ye dumplin'. It's somethin' that's best pals wi' a fowil feend an' hates peelgreems.'

For the rest of the hymn, the lad and me mumbled words of verses that we didn't know and couldn't understand, but when it came to the last line of every verse, we gave it our all while the tears ran down our cheeks: 'TOOO BEE A PEEELGREEEEM.' Our spotty neighbour in the primary-school uniform looked at us with total disdain, which made us convulse all the more.

At last the blessings and the addresses and the hymns were finished. The brown lad and me dried our cheeks, and everybody settled down, while another cloaked figure strode to the microphone and placed a large sheaf of papers on the lectern. This guy was at least six foot two, thin, round-shouldered and one of the fur-lined hood varieties. He flicked out his elbows under his heavy cloak so that it would settle more comfortably around his shoulders. In that instant, he looked for all the world like a vulture that had just landed on a half-eaten carcass as he slowly surveyed the rows of tender children before him. For a full five seconds he just stood there, letting the majesty of his black robe and his cold vulture eyes do the business. I'd seen old grainy newsreels at the pictures of Adolf Hitler at carefully choreographed rallies, where he did a very similar act before he started fervently convincing thousands and thousands of his faithful followers that they were entitled to rule the planet. But that was at the pictures; this man was a big black vulture who was not twenty yards away from my twelve-year-old person, and this felt a whole heap more sinister.

He introduced himself as Dr Morrison, the deputy rector. I could detect the soft, menacing Gallic lilt of the Western Isles in his voice, and swore silently to myself that this was somebody I was going to stay well away from. Herr Dr Morrison began to whisper out kids' names and allocate each to designated areas of the assembly hall where big cardboard signs had magically appeared bearing the letters 'A', 'B', 'C' and 'F'. As far as I could understand, each letter represented a different class. 'A' was for kids who were expected to get at least O levels and possibly Highers. The 'B' area was for children who had been judged to have a good chance of getting a couple of O levels and certainly a General School Leaving Certificate, whereas 'C' was for kids who didn't have any real academic ability and were expected to feed the factories, building sites and shipyards with labourers and semi-skilled operators. 'F' catered for the torn T-shirts and battered sandshoes. Most of these people had real learning difficulties and shouldn't have been there at all. The new enlightened system made sure we were all given an equal chance to achieve our fifteen minutes of fame.

The spectacle had begun in the last couple of weeks at primary school, when the headmaster came into the class and read out the results of our 11-Plus Exam – the 'qualy'. Four alternatives had been available to the educational mandarins: senior secondary, junior secondary, lower junior secondary and the dreaded modified section, the 'moddy'. Based on the exams and questionable IQ tests, we had taken months before, our whole future was now to be decided for us. So me, the brown lad, the spotty uniformed girl, Findus the Fisherman and everybody else watched as hundreds of children were publicly separated into four categories: the 'university potential', the 'trades-school potential', the 'unskilled-worker potential' and the 'no potential at all'.

Through the sounds of shuffling feet, scraping chairs and murmuring gossip, I listened as surnames were read out in alphabetical order, edging ever closer to 'R' for 'Robertson': 'Brian Malcolm, area F . . . Dorothy McGregor, area B.' Then Morrison quietly announced, 'Gordon McKinley, area A.' The lad next to me got up, nodded at me and began to shuffle his way along the row of chairs on his way to the area marked 'A'.

At primary school, I'd been a big fish, even a bit of a smart-arse Jack the Lad. I knew everybody and everybody knew me, and I was even revered among the lads as being one of the best fighters in our class. Here I was, though, becoming increasingly isolated and unsure. This wasn't at all what I'd bargained for. Even my new brown buddy had left and I was alone in my little chair in the middle of a chrome and pine holiday camp. Just as I was starting to feel really sorry for my poor wee self, the doctor's soft, lilting voice proclaimed, 'William Robertson, area A.'

Gordon McKinley beamed a great big smile at me as I bumped my way between the chairs to area A. 'Hey, pal,' he said, as I joined him. 'Fancy us bein' in the same group, eh?'

I smiled an equally broad, relieved smile back at

him: you can always tell when you just 'click' with somebody, and I knew that we were destined to be great friends.

The words came fast and furious now in our anxiety to re-establish the contact made during the giggling hymn. 'Ye'll be Goardin?' I said. 'Ah heard yer name ca'd oot by the big lad wi' the black goon.'

'An' ye're Wulliam. Ah heard him an' a'.'

'Aye, but Ah get ca'd Wullie, an' Ah hope ye're no' a hobgoblin, 'cos Ah'm thinkin' o' becomin' a peelgreem.'

We started to chuckle, and, as both of us half turned round to see if anybody we knew was being allocated to our group, a wave of the stupid childish giggling fits washed over us again, because a big, spotty, disgusted, primary-school uniform had just joined our area. We later learned that her name was Margaret (Muggie) Strachan and she lived in a stone semi-detached bungalow in the original little village of Kirkton. She was desperate to show that she detested the riff-raff invasion that had swamped her parents' world in a tidal wave of council houses, and she looked down on me and my new brown mate with utter revulsion. Neither of us could know then that she would be the very first girl I would kiss on the lips and that hers would be the first breasts that I would be allowed to tremblingly fondle.

'So how come ye're sae broon, Goardin?'

'Ma mum an' dad live in India, Wullie, an' Ah wiz there fur twa months jist afore Ah came here tae the skael.'

I'd never met anybody who had been to England, never mind India, so I was overwhelmed with admiration and couldn't get enough of the details of what it was to be an international traveller. 'Did ye go on a plane?', 'Whit's it like?', 'Did ye go above the clouds?', 'Whit's it like?', 'Whar d'ye live now if yer mum an' dad's in India?', 'Whit's it like in India?', 'Is it dead hot?', 'An' did ye get that broon in jist twa months?' For the next ten minutes or so, Dr Morrison's soft voice continued to direct children to their respective locations, but I didn't care who else joined our group; I was hypnotised by Gordon's amazing story, which just seemed to get better and better.

'My mum's Indian,' he said. 'That's the reason how ma skin's a wee bit broon.'

This was more amazing than a story from a comic, and here was me in the middle of it. 'Nae kiddin'? Did ye grow up in India, then?'

Gordon nodded.

'That's brilliant. Imagine haein' an Indian mum – that's brilliant. Can yer mum speak Inglish as good as us, or diz she speak Indian? Can you speak Indian, Goardin?'

I could have spent the rest of the day exploring my

new friend's amazing life, but suddenly we were all called to order and asked to form lines. Each contingent was led to a separate area of our huge new school, and Gordon, primary-school-uniform girl, myself and the other seventy or so members of the A team followed the back of four black gowns along wide corridors filled with the bright daylight that streamed in through acres of glass and gleamed along smooth pastel-coloured walls. This wasn't a school at all: schools were little and dark and smelled of industrial polish and damp woollen gloves drying on thick heating pipes. This place was new and bright and smelled of fresh paint and varnish.

After walking for about eleven miles through a Dulux colour chart of corridors, one of the black cloaks opened a set of double glass doors and us lemmings spilled out on to a wide open area of concrete slabs. Gordon and me stuck close together in the middle of the throng, blinking in the sunlight. The wide square was surrounded on three sides by buildings, while the fourth side opened out on to what looked like a municipal park, with lush green grass to the horizon and little fresh trees tied to stakes.

To our right and left, sheer cliffs of glass windows and pastel-coloured plastic panels rose three floors above our heads. Every shining block we could see had a flat roof, even the soaring five-storey tower that housed the huge assembly hall where we had started out looked like it had been scalped by an eighty-foot Apache. We all milled about like before, trying to recognise familiar faces from our primary schools. Gordon and me stayed together, although between us we only picked up about seven or eight of our former classmates, and stood in a little group waiting to see what would happen. The four black-cloaked teachers were standing in a huddle near the door, looking at sheaves of paper. Then they nodded to each other and one of them stepped forward and called above the babble for silence. This guy had a fur-lined cape – he must be important, so silence prevailed.

For the next twenty minutes or so, we went through a mini version of what had happened in the main assembly hall. Pupils were allocated their class for the next year, ranging from A1 to A4. A1 was for '*la crème de la crème*', who were the brightest and best in the school. I was allocated to A4, which was the 'just made it to the A section by the skin of your teeth' class. Somewhere in a distant part of the pastel-coated palace another group was being allocated to their class within the F team, from F1, or the 'nearly made it to a C' class, down to F4, which was of course for '*la* scum *de la* scum'.

Class A4 began to emerge as the best place to be as two of the more adventurous of my old primary friends and then, thankfully, my new friend Gordon were allocated to the group. Three of Gordon's former classmates, together with a whole other heap of strangers and the uniformed Miss Muggie Strachan, were sent to swell our ranks before we were marched off by our very own non-fur-lined black cloak.

He was called Mr Soutar, and was a boyish man in his early twenties who looked as if he became a beatnik at weekends. He told us that he was to be our register teacher for the next year, which meant that we had to turn up to this particular classroom every morning so that he could check if anybody was absent. He then read out our names from his book and marked each time a pupil responded. Having counted us all in, he informed us that, as our register teacher, part of his role was to help us if we had any problems or concerns. This wasn't right at all – teachers were there to teach you things and hit you across your outstretched hands with a thick leather belt to make sure you behaved; nobody had ever said anything about coming to them with concerns. This Soutar might even turn out to be a good guy.

Mind you, anything would be a breath of fresh air after Miss Montieth, the evil little dwarf who had called herself an 'educator' and 'educated' the senior class of eleven-year-olds at my former primary school. She had taught children all her long life, and was deeply frustrated that legislation had been introduced after the First World War that prevented her from thrashing her charges with a birch rod. All she had now was her leather belt and her poisonous tongue, both of which she used liberally, especially on boys.

Her crowning educational achievement, though, had to be when she tried to assist David Barrowman to overcome his speech impediment. Davie had a profound stutter, which was made ten times worse whenever he had to speak in front of the class. Miss Montieth decided that the best cure for Davie's 'affliction' was to make him confront his problems head-on, sort of an early version of modern aversion therapy, and she picked on the poor wee soul mercilessly to answer questions, or read things off the blackboard, or whenever any opportunity arose to expose him to his nightmare of public speaking. He would stand there almost choking as he tried his very best to get a word together, only managing 'Th– th– th– tha– th–' while the ever-helpful 'educator' poked him in the arm with her index finger, saying, 'Come on, come on now, say it, David.' Even at that age I knew this wasn't right, and some of the girls in the class had to wipe their eyes when Davie was inevitably and ignominiously told to sit down.

Soutar, however, was almost chatty, and he sat on his desk like a mate. 'This new school of ours has huge potential, boys and girls, but it needs a big effort from us all if we're going to realise that potential. For example, we don't have a school badge, or a motto, or even school colours, so one of the first things we have to do is collect enough money to have our badge and motto formally registered with the Lord Lyon King of Arms, who is responsible for protecting the heraldic tradition of Scotland. If we all bring in thruppence every week, we'll have our school badge and colours registered by Christmas.' He positively beamed at the thought.

I didn't know if this Lord Lyon King of Arms was a real person, a symbolic idea or even a mythical creature that lived on an iceberg, but one thing I did know was that he wasn't getting thruppence a week off me. If you're called Lord, you've had generations of getting money out of ordinary punters. Let Lord Lyon pay for Kirkton High's badge.

'Come back tae ma hoose fur yer tea, Goardin. Ah'll tell ma mum that ye're a peelgreem that's been attacked by a Lord Lyon an' a hobgoblin. She'll gie us bacon an' egg an' chips.'

Chapter Five

The Big Fight

*Real courage is facing your demons
when all help is gone.*

One of the areas where we collected money on Saturday morning would now be described as an 'area of multiple social deprivation'. Beechwood is the kind of name that modern property developers give to upmarket housing developments in Kingston-upon-Thames, but we knew Beechwood as the Dundee council estate that most of the whores, criminals, benefit fraudsters, nutters, drunks and comic singers of Dundee called home.

The sad thing about a place like that is the majority of ordinary people are trying to make a decent home and a life for themselves and their kids, while swimming against the tide of mayhem caused by the mindless few. And there doesn't seem to be anybody helping them.

One particular incident summed up the place for me. Every day for about the first three or four weeks that I worked on the round, I dutifully deposited two pints of milk on the doorstep of a seemingly deserted ground-floor flat. Slowly, it began to dawn on me that there were never any empty bottles to be collected, although the full bottles disappeared into the house every morning. I just shrugged it off and trotted with my wire carrier to the next-door delivery. One Friday night when I knocked on the door to collect the DSS (Department of Health and Social Security) milk tokens as usual, the woman of the house asked me to step inside.

'Ah'm gled Ah caught ye, son. We need ye tae collect a few bottles fur us.' She opened the door to the bathroom, leading off the hall.

I had already taken a full stride into the bathroom before a nauseating wall of sensory horror hit my nostrils and tastebuds. The bath was filled almost to the top with four weeks' supply of unwashed empty milk bottles.

'Could ye jist git rid o' them fur us, son?' Her voice was matter-of-fact, as if she were asking me to remember to close the door as I left.

My skin began to crawl and I thought I was going to be sick. I needed air and instinctively backed out into the hall. As I bolted, retching, for the front door, I managed to leave her in no doubt that I wouldn't be complying with her request. 'That'll be fuckin' richt. Ye can stick the whole lot up yer arse.'

When I told Avril, she immediately put a thick pencil line through the name in her book. 'Right, Wullie, that's one less on yer roond.'

For all I know or care, the woman and her bottles are still there.

My grannie Robertson might have made a small difference, though, even in Beechwood, through the kindness and caring she radiated every day. When my grannie lived in a tenement slum in the West Port area of Dundee, an entrepreneur lived above her in a tiny, sparsely furnished two-room flat. This lady worked from home entertaining guests, mostly in the late evenings, and my grannie was always trying to lead her 'back to the light' by telling her that the Lord Jesus would help her if only she would put her faith in him. Wee Grannie wasn't a Bible-thumping zealot or a loud evangelist; she just wouldn't walk past on the other side of the road when someone was unhappy or suffering. She saw everybody around her as being good at heart, while recognising that some poor souls were 'lost in the wilderness', like misguided children.

One evening, her professional, self-employed

upstairs neighbour was unburdening herself over a cup of tea and a few Embassy fags. Business was dreadful. She had nothing in the cupboard, neither food nor gin. She was at her wits' end. My grannie did what she always did in situations like this. 'Let's baith o' us git doon on oor knees an' ask the Lamb o' God tae come tae the rescue o' anithir wee lost lamb.' So they both knelt in my grannie's little living room and asked Jesus to 'tak' into his airums, oor sister Jessie – a sinner but a good wummin wi' a kind hert'.

'Oor Saviour will protect ye an' provide fur ye, Jessie. Jist hae faith.'

Half an hour after the impromptu prayer meeting on the linoleum, there was a frantic knocking at my grannie's door and a beaming Jessie burst into the room. 'Ye wiz right a' the time, Dolly,' she panted. 'The Lord diz miraquilisly provide, jist like ye said. It wiz jist like a' they stories ye telt me aboot the three fishes an' the sivin loaves, ken? Ah'd jist got back upstairs tae the hoose, still thinkin' aboot oor prayer, when the Lord Jesus answered oor plea, providin' fur me an' workin' in mysteerius ways, jist like ye said.

'Suddinly, there wiz a wee knock at the door, an' guess whit, Dolly? Guess whit? It wiz ma best gentleman customer. Ma very best gentleman, Dolly. Oh, Dolly, the Lord Jesus must hae sent him efter oor prayers. He gae me fehv pound, Dolly, fehv whole pound. Hae ane o' ma fags. Ah'm goin' tae pray tae Jesus mair often.

Hae anithir fag, Dolly. Wid ye like a fish supper?'

After the slums of the West Port were eventually demolished and the people rehoused, Jessie probably continued to deliver her innocent prayers for more customers, on bended knee in a top flat in Beechwood.

To be on the safe side, we always collected the money in pairs in Beechwood, and Si and Wee John were one of the teams that worked the closes in the four-storey blocks where the stair lights never worked. There were eight flats in these closes, so it made sense for one boy to collect money from customers on the top two floors, while the other lad collected from customers on the bottom two.

In one of the blocks where Fletcher's had customers in all eight flats, the schedule needed Wee John to collect from the top floors and Si to do the bottom ones, while the rest of us except Gordon stood on the lorry jeering about how long they were taking. It wasn't that Gordon was averse to jeering; it was just that he was the only other boy who also had to collect money at this point in the round, and his customer was an elderly woman who lived alone in a ground-floor flat in the close directly opposite the one that Si and Wee John had just disappeared into. She and her now-deceased husband must have been among the original occupants of Beechwood before the place became a menagerie, because she was still trying to maintain a little outpost of the civilised world among the back greens and closes where Attila the Hun and all his tribe now roamed unchallenged. She was fighting a losing battle, though, and was obviously terrified even to open her door to the close, because Gordon was instructed to deliver one pint of milk to her ground-floor windowsill every second morning except Sunday, which meant she got three pints of milk a week without having to open the door. He collected the empty bottles and the money from the same window, where she would give him two shillings for the milk money and a penny tip. The penny tip bought her one of her few direct contacts with somebody from the outside world, but it also bought for us the only collection point in Beechwood where the payment transaction took place in full view of all the people on the lorry, and so was the only time a laddie could collect on his own and feel safe.

Wee Good John was little but he was fast, so he always reached the second-floor landing about half a flight of stairs ahead of Si. One Saturday, as he turned the corner of the landing, he ran straight into a bloke who was standing on the stairs, and after the briefest of pauses and, 'Sorry, pal, Ah didnae see ye,' he was off up the next flight. Si arrived a few seconds later and went to knock on the first door when a blinding pain burst in the back of his head. Luckily, he didn't lose consciousness completely or the bloke would have had his money pouch and been clean away. Dreaming of untold riches, the villain had waited in the cold stairwell for Si and smacked him on the head with a wooden baton when his back was turned. The guy had probably spent hours hiding in the dark 'casing the joint' to find out who went where to collect the money. If he'd spoken to Avril or Auld Jim, he might have got a start on the round the next time somebody left, but the prospect of becoming actively involved in milk delivery, or any other meaningful work, must have convinced him that being a 'footpad' was a better career choice.

What the stupid prick didn't realise, though, was that most of the residents of Beechwood paid for their milk with little green tokens they got from the DSS, affectionately known as the 'Soashul', so we took in very little in the way of actual money. Besides, we had to give any pound- or ten-shilling notes we got to Avril every time we came back to the truck, so the little leather purse we carried only contained our tips and enough coins to give people change.

After the blow, Si fell against the close wall, slowly losing it but with still enough savvy to realise he needed help quickly, so he screamed out to Wee John two floors above. We heard the screaming from the back of the lorry and all tore off into the close, bounding up the stairs three at a time.

I arrived on the landing just behind Steevie and stopped dead in my tracks. I couldn't believe my eyes: Wee John was like a demented mother gerbil protecting her young; he'd clearly decided to die like a Viking, sword in hand, and was flailing at the bloke like a madman. Si's assailant was actually backing away, completely thrown off guard at being attacked head-on by a rampant stick insect. When he saw the Seventh Cavalry arriving, he quickly realised that he was now the one who was in grave danger, so he got back in the real world and whacked Wee John in the stomach. Normally, a fist into Wee John's stomach would have gone right through his little body and come out the back, but he was giving such a good impression of a whirling dervish that the blow barely struck its intended target and glanced across his midriff. Nevertheless, Wee John instantly folded in half and dropped like a whore's drawers.

Thankfully, Wee Good John's courage and selfless-ness had bought us the time we needed and the writing was on the wall for Dick Turpin. Hardly break-ing stride, Steevie leaped forward and swung at the bloke's head with the empty milk bottle he'd brought with him – 'Ma wee insurance policy, ye see.' Although the guy easily blocked the blow with his left arm, he still had one eye on Steevie and his wee insurance policy as he turned his head away from the shot and towards me as I was coming forward, so I found my forehead about ten inches from his undefended nose. It was more instinctive reaction than martial expertise; I headered into his face just like you header a crossed ball into the goal, and nutted through the bridge of his nose. I felt the bone and cartilage splinter and he yelped like a scalded cat as his head jerked away from the pain and he staggered backwards against the wall.

Enter film-star Johnny. He skipped forward and smacked the bloke with a textbook right hook that landed on his already broken nose with a sound like the crack of a rifle shot. The guy's nose exploded in a volcano of blood and snot as the punch drove the back of his head into the close wall. Just in case there were any hidden cameras or Hollywood talent scouts in the close, Johnny flexed his arms and danced backwards like a world champ looking dead cool.

At this point, Fat Boab arrived wheezing up the stairs 'in the nick o' time' and saw a man in his early twenties leaning against the landing wall with blood pouring from what used to be his nose and his legs instinctively spread wide trying to maintain his failing balance. Well, these kinds of fight opportunities are what dreams are made of, so Boab delivered the *coup de grâce* with a sickening toe-ender square into the bloke's balls. The guy's knees jerked together and he pitched forward on to his face, lying there motionless while his blood and vomit formed a widening pool on the landing.

He was finished. He was in the twilight zone with his face, head and groin in a real mess, but this wasn't retribution enough for Fat Boab when he looked over at Si sitting against the wall with blood oozing from the back of his head, staining his hair, his shirt and the close wall, and at Wee John kneeling on the landing retching like a half-drowned rat. The normally placid Boab became a shark in a feeding frenzy. 'You fuckin' bastard!' he screamed. 'See how good it feels now, ye fuckin' fucker,' and he started kicking and stamping all kinds of shit out of the crumpled form on the landing. I think he might have permanently injured or even killed the bloke if it hadn't been for Si, who, having now partially recovered his senses, pulled himself up on to his knees, leaned over the body on the deck and said in a bad New York accent, 'You have the right to remain silent and the right to an attorney.' We all erupted in a fit of laughter and relief, which snapped Boab out of his bloodlust and took the heat out of the moment. Only Steevie didn't seem to get the joke and, streetwise and opportunistic as always, got down on his knees beside Si and began to go through the guy's pockets. He was delighted with his booty of two and fourpence and an almost full tin of tobacco.

Suddenly, reality arrived in the shape of Avril. 'Git the hell oot o' this, all o' yez, afore the boabies git here. Wullie, Johnny, pull that bastard doon the stairs a wee bit so it looks like he fell.'

Fell? Aye, right, Avril. I could just hear PC Murdoch giving his report to the sergeant back at the nick: 'It was a most terrible accident, you see. The poor man obviously fell doon the stairs, bounced off every wall in

the close an' ended up smashin' his face into his balls.'
Nevertheless, me and Johnny dragged the guy to a
position where we thought he would have ended up if
he'd accidentally fallen, and left him there marinating
in a puddle of his own bodily fluids.

As we turned to make good our escape, I noticed a
small wooden baton that Steevie had slid out from the
inside pocket of the guy's jerkin and quickly discarded
as being of no commercial value. It was a miniature
baseball bat about a foot long with the words 'New York
Yankees' written down the side, obviously the instrument he'd used to smack Si. I lifted it as a memento of
New York and our morning's entertainment.

When we reached the mouth of the close, Avril and
the lads were already in their places on the back of the
lorry – all except for Gordon, who was waiting on the
pavement, having crossed the road from his windowsill
after hearing the commotion. As me and Johnny
bolted out of the close, Gordon theatrically bent his
knees, did a music-hall adjustment of his goolies, said,
'Evenin' all,' and then slowly walked towards the lorry
with his thumbs under his armpits singing the theme
tune from the popular TV series of the time *Dixon of
Dock Green*, 'an ordinary copper who's patrolling his
beat'.

Si was on the lorry right enough, but he clearly
wasn't in the same time zone as the rest of us. His face
was deathly white and he had congealed blood all over

the back of his head and down his jerkin. He was swaying so much that Fat Boab had to use his bulk to squash him against the rail to stop him toppling off the platform, and even Steevie looked up from his plunder to offer, 'It's a good joab it wiz yer heid, Si. Ye've got that much brains they wid bend the boy's club.'

Meanwhile, Wee John was hanging off the far end of the platform, being completely ignored by everyone and trying to be sick. It was obvious to all of us except Steevie that Si needed some serious medical attention.

Avril looked genuinely concerned. 'Are ye feelin' awright, son?' she said. 'Come an' sit doon beside me on the flair here. Ye're no' lookin' that great. Ye should mibbie go an' git yersel' seen tae.' After a few moments looking at Si's swirling eyeballs, she made her momentous decision and issued the international milk-delivery distress call by picking an empty bottle out of a crate and banging it three times on the flatbed floor of the truck.

The lorry came to a quick but controlled stop, the driver's door opened, and the legendary Jim Fletcher got slowly down from his cab. It was the first time that I knew for certain that Auld Jim had legs, because I had never seen him standing outside the truck; in fact, I had always thought he was a design feature that Bedford had included as an optional extra on this model.

Avril stated her case. 'This laddie has a split heid an' he needs tae go tae the infirmary now, Dad.'

Jim looked at Si and snorted. 'Awright, lass, if ye think so. We'll be up near the infirmary in aboot twenty meenits,' and he turned back to his cab.

'No, Dad.' Avril was now cradling Si in her arms. 'This laddie's got kingcusshin an' he canna wait till we feenish the next bit o' the roond – he has tae git there now.'

Jim stood in the road and glared at Avril, and for a few seconds it could have gone either way. 'Richt,' he said. 'Richt ye are,' and he vaulted back into the cab.

The lorry screamed off up the road with all of us holding on for dear life, Avril trying to protect Si's head from banging on the floor and Johnny telling us all to get hold of the crates to stop them sliding over the side. We had only gone about five hundred yards when the lorry braked to a sedate twenty-five miles an hour, and we all smiled sweetly at the flashing lights of the cop car that roared past us in the opposite direction. It seemed that somebody living in the close had a phone after all.

I briefly wondered if they would actually be daft enough to conclude that the guy had fallen down the stairs, but then reality came calling and I started to giggle. 'They must be on their way tae an accident, lads, tearin' alang like that. Mibbie some poor soul fell doon stairs somewhere.'

Johnny piped up, 'Nae, Wullie, if some poor bastard had fell doon stairs, we wid hae seen him. Did ony o' you lads see an arsehole wi' bashed-in ba's lyin' in a close this moarnin'?'

The nervous giggling started to take over as we tried to make light of what we had done, while the truck accelerated up to nearly fifty miles an hour through the deserted streets on its way to the Dundee Royal Infirmary.

About a quarter-mile further on, another set of flashing lights came hurtling towards us on their way to the crime scene. This time it was only an ambulance, so Jim kept his foot hard to the floor and we whipped past each other like the Red Arrows display team.

I briefly caught sight of the ambulance driver's bemused face trying to work out why a fully laden milk truck was heading somewhere faster than he was. I'm sure he must have imagined one of his colleagues kneeling over a traumatised patient somewhere up the road and earnestly saying, 'Jist hold on fur a wee bit langer, missus. The para mulk laddies will be here ony minute an' ye'll get as much mulk in yer tea as ye kin drink. Hold ma hand, missus. Ye'll hae mulk in yer porridge this moarnin'. Ah gie ye ma word.'

We stopped about twenty yards from the entrance to the infirmary, just out of sight of the main door.

Jim got out of his cab and walked to the back of the lorry. 'Whit's the laddie's name, Avril?' he whispered in a whisky-flavoured voice we could all smell.

'He gits ca'd Si, Dad, but his real name's Russell.'

Jim looked around him, frustrated and confused. 'Then how the hell diz he git ca'd Si?'

Avril lost her rag. 'Whit the hell diz it metter whit he gits ca'd? Jist git him aff the larry an' intae the casualty.'

Jim began mumbling to himself, stomped around to the little platform at the back of the truck, and looked up at us.

Fat Boab lifted Si down on to the road. 'Here he is, Jim. This is him, an' he's goin' tae need some stitches in his heid. It's still bleedin' a bit, Jim.'

Auld Jim put his arm round Si and motioned him towards the entrance to the hospital. 'Ye're a good laddie. Jist walk intae the cashulty an' tell them that ye wiz oot gettin' moarnin' papers fur yer mum an' ye slipped an' fell an' split yer heid. Dinna say onythin' aboot deliverin' mulk or we'll a' be speakin' tae the boabies fur weeks. D'ye understand, Simon . . . er, Si . . . or . . . er, Russell?'

We all watched Si walking unsteadily towards the main entrance of the hospital. As soon as he turned into the main courtyard, Jim revved the engine and we sped off back to the delivery round to make up for lost time.

'Ye done really great there, wee man.' Unbelievably, Johnny had his arm round Wee John's shoulder and was helping him to straighten up. 'Ye showed that big shite that he couldnae mess wi' us, eh? Well done, John Boy, ye done great.'

This was like Elvis telling some wee punter that he looked really cool, so it took a few moments for us all to accept that it was actually happening. But it needed Johnny's words to remind us that it was Wee Good John's bravery that had saved Si from being much more seriously hurt.

Fat Boab was the first to echo Johnny's sentiments. 'Ye were fuckin' brilliant, John. We should hae a' jist stayed on the larry. Ye could hae took him yersel'. Better no' get on the wrong side o' you, eh?' Fat Boab said with mock deference. 'Ye're a demon when ye get roused.'

We all agreed, shouted abuse, said that we never knew he was such a killer, and made jokes about dark horses. The lorry was at least twenty miles an hour above the speed limit now and the milk bottles rattled in their crates as Auld Jim tried to make up precious seconds and resume deliveries. I stood on the little platform with both hands on the huddin' rail, smiling at Wee Good John being clapped on the shoulder by Elvis, while the rest heaped praises on his head. He was standing straight as a guardsman, his bruised guts and the bile in his mouth forgotten, and for a few brief glorious minutes, John Murray was as close as he would ever get to being Big Bad John.

Chapter Six

At the Berries

'There's nae stanes in *ma* luggie.'

Gordon, Wee John and me sat among little mounds of freshly mown grass on the edge of Dundee's ring road, munching peas licked straight from their crunchy green pods. The three of us were surrounded by piles of Dundee Town Council's grass cuttings and farmers' empty pods, and we soaked in the smell of grass and peas while the summer sun warmed our bare backs.

During the glorious days of the school summer holidays, known to all as 'the sivin weekees', Gordon, Wee Good and me were among the worst culprits for robbing berries and peas from tractors, and would arrange to meet at the side of the Kingsway for a couple of hours' feasting after we'd finished our milk round. Sometimes Si and Steevie and a few non-milk laddies from school joined us. Si would usually bring his wee sister, although she was never allowed anywhere near the business end of the operation, and the two of them always took most of their plunder home. We all knew it would form part of the family evening meal.

Steevie, on the other hand, just revelled in the thieving, and I don't think he even liked raspberries or fresh peas that much. Johnny never came with us because what we were doing wasn't nearly cool enough for his image, and since there were no women tractor drivers, what was the point? Fat Boab's strict Presbyterian code wouldn't have condoned the stealing of even a solitary pea, so he was never there either. Besides, he probably couldn't have moved his bulk smartly enough to avoid being whacked by a tractor.

From about mid-July until the end of August, thousands of tons of fresh strawberries, raspberries, peas and other goodies poured along this highway on massive trailers towed by huge, slow tractors, like a line of giant mutant worker ants. The raspberry and strawberry trailers were sometimes piled a bit too high, making it possible to shove a long, thin tree branch into the upper layers of the passing stacked punnets and, with a bit of luck, dislodge a few off the back. This trick didn't work very often, but if your stick happened to catch the tightly packed punnets in the right place, it was simply a case of scooping up the piles of berries that landed on the tarmac as the leviathan tractor lumbered on. We were a bit like crocodiles waiting for the vast herds of migrating wildebeest to cross some river in the Transvaal. The tractor drivers knew we would pick off a few exposed unfortunates, but it meant very little to the integrity of the herd. The huge, juicy, red mass swept on.

Fresh peas were much easier plunder. The pea tractors were faster and their trailers were smaller, but they positively dripped with newly harvested little green delicacies on their way to the Smedley processing factory outside Broughty Ferry. It wasn't just pods they were carrying; each trailer was stacked high with what looked like a quarter-acre's worth of cultivated vegetation, as if half a field had been ruthlessly torn from the ground that very morning by the pillaging Viking hordes of King Norsenpod 'the Pea-Taker' and thrown, screaming in dying piles, on to a fleet of flatbed trailers. Many pods were still twitching in their death throes as we liberated them from the horrors of being canned.

Most of the young tractor drivers gunning their engines along the dual carriageway seemed to think they were piloting a cutting-edge Formula One racing car, even though they were pulling a haystack of pea plants behind them. Towing ten tons of vegetation on a flatbed trailer behind your Ferrari wouldn't exactly improve your odds for the Monaco Grand Prix with the bookies, but these lads didn't seem to realise or care. That suited us fine, because the faster these racing-driver champions drove their tractors, the easier it was for us. A simple tree branch might keep you in a moderate supply of raspberries and strawberries for the day, but for the sweet taste of peas fresh from the pod, you needed something far more sophisticated: a garden rake.

All you had to do was stand at the edge of the carriageway, wait for Stirling Moss to come along in his tractor with its 'go faster through the cow shit' stripes, then force the rake hard into the peas as the trailer whizzed past. The rake scraped along the side of the stack and dragged a pile of fresh stalks and pods on to the edge of the road, to be consumed at leisure on the grass verge while you waited for the next victim. It probably wasn't cost-effective for the drivers to stop, and they wouldn't have caught us, anyway, so they just shook their fists and snarled at us from the cab, while we smiled back and happily carried on.

It wasn't all plain sailing, though. If your rake went in too deep, it could get wedged in the tangle of pea plants and wrenched from your grasp. Or, worse, if you held on too tightly, you could be pulled under the back wheels of the trailer. We all became quite skilled at knowing the optimum angle at which a rake would maximise the pea count without getting stuck and, more importantly, when to let go in an emergency. Si had probably worked it out in his bedroom using trigonometry or something, but for the rest of us, it was all in the sensitive vibration of the rake handle and the subtle variations in the sounds of the pea plants being dragged off the back. I suppose concert violinists experience similar sensations.

'Ken whut, lads? We should go tae the berries this week.'

I had just about finished decoding Wee John's semi-mashed pea-green mouthful when Gordon responded on behalf of us both. 'How the fuck wid we want tae go tae the berries, Wee Good? We've got mair money than we need.'

Wee John laughed out loud. ''Cos it's mair fun than sittin' on oor arses on the Kingsway scoffin' berries an' peas. It'll be a laugh. A'body else goes, eh? We'll ask Si an' his wee sister an' Fat Boab tae come an' a'. Fuck the money. It'll be great.'

Wee Good John and me looked at each other like naughty children sharing a joke. Like most Dundee kids, we'd been to the berries every summer since we were about ten, usually earning less than the cost of our packed lunch, and we knew what would be in store. Only Gordon would be entering unfamiliar territory. Wee Good John was right: it would be a laugh.

For five or six weeks every summer, half of Dundee's schoolchildren formed part of a huge daily migration into the countryside to pick berries. The summer of 1963 was just one more wee coin in a wishing well that had been in existence for more than a hundred years, because during July and August almost all of the remarkably fertile farmland of Scotland's east coast hung ripe with soft fruit that the kids of the city, and every other town and village in the area, were only too willing to be paid to harvest.

Acre upon acre and row upon endless row of succulent red raspberries, strawberries and bright green peas covered every available square foot of arable farmland within a twenty-mile radius of the town. Prairies of berries and peas engulfed most of the Carse of Gowrie along both banks of the River Tay from Dundee to Perth, then flowed northwards over Blairgowrie and into the hills beyond. The overwhelming crimson and green tide rolled up the valley of the Howe o' the Mearns on the eastern fringes of the North Sea as far as Stonehaven, where local schoolchildren and other more professional pickers fell upon it like a biblical plague of locusts.

The bounty was picked daily by an army of schoolkids, Irish migrant workers and everyday Dundee punters who may or may not have been claiming unemployment payouts or invalidity benefit. Whole families even spent their summer holidays at the berries, living in caravans parked near the fields. The result of their combined labours was transported from the farms to the canning and jam-making plants and the distribution warehouses on the eastern fringes of Dundee and beyond. Regardless of its place of origin, every single pea and berry seemed to end up being hauled along the same vehicular artery: the Kingsway.

The morning after Wee John's suggestion, he, Gordon, Steevie, Si, his wee sister, Fat Boab, the Turnbull twins, my wee brother Ian and me pedalled along the Kingsway in the opposite direction to the drone of tractors. All the milk laddies had finished their round, eaten breakfast, and made up sandwiches. The Turnbull boys stayed in bed till the last minute and a wee bit longer, knowing that their mum would have everything prepared and organised for their day. Big mistake.

Normally, we would never go anywhere with a twelve-year-old girl, like Si's younger sister. Girls were the biggest pain in the arse imaginable because they slowed you down, got hurt, cried, told the teacher on you, and generally bleated and fucked up your world. Si's wee sister was different, though. She wasn't a girl; she was Si's wee sister, and as such got included in most of the things that the milk laddies did. She screamed and laughed out loud on the morning when we pulled her on to the step to become an honorary milk laddie.

The two minutes' driving towards the depot was enough: she wanted to become the very first milk lassie. I had allowed my brother Ian to come with us in the hope that the two twelve-year-olds would keep each other company.

We were heading for the berry fields north of Birkhill, about five miles outside Dundee, where we knew we'd all get a start because the berries picked there went for things like jam, flavouring and dye. Raspberries for the table or for fancy wee cakes were mostly grown on other farms further from the town, and were picked by professional 'clean-pickers', who delicately plucked every individual raspberry from its plant, leaving behind just a clean white husk. Scruffy Dundee schoolkids would never be allowed anywhere near the fields where the table berries grew, because our technique was a bit less dexterous. We simply ripped the fruit from the plant as fast as our fingers could move, and if a few husks, bits of stock, flies or even leaves got in among the mush, the berry juice would soon camouflage the offending articles.

Most farmers supplied 'berry buses' to transport city pickers to and from the fields. These vehicles had invariably been rejected by the Bolivian National Pig Farmers' Cooperative as being 'too dilapidated and unroadworthy for our current requirements', and they always smelled overpoweringly of stale raspberry juice and sweat mixed with Capstan 'Full-Strength' fags.

That's one of the reasons why we were cycling.

Despite all his riches from the milk, Gordon was the only one among us who didn't have access to a bike. Even Si's wee sister had a boy's cycle that was once her big brother's, and Si himself had an old black-framed relic that had belonged to his dad before he pissed off. Gordon's lack of two-wheeled transport came as a bit of a shock when he first told me, because almost every boy gets a bike from Santa sooner or later, even if it's only a second-hand cleaned-up one, the variety that Santa seemed to favour in working-class Britain in the 1960s. In Gordon's case, however, Santa had been stuck in a snow drift somewhere near Chittagong, so all the rest of us had bikes that could get us at least as far as Birkhill, while Gordon had kukri knives, amputated elephant's feet and weird stuffed crocodiles. Luckily, Brian McLaren's big brother came to the rescue and magnanimously offered to rent his bike to Gordon at only a shilling for the whole day, a never-to-be-repeated opportunity. The milk laddies put in tuppence each, so Gordon only had to pay fourpence.

We arrived at the fields and chained our bikes together. The berry gaffer started us all right away, after a couple of sceptical glances at my wee brother and Si's wee sister, and we were split into pairs. Each pair was issued with one big galvanised pail like Oor Wullie sits on and a small personal bucket, inexplicably called a 'luggie'. Then the whole troop of us was shown to the rows, or 'dreels', of bushes we were to pick.

Most of us started threading our belt through the handle of the luggie so it hung from our waist, leaving both hands free to pick. Steevie, however, sat down with his back to the bushes, put his luggie by his side, lit one of his revolting little nippers, and said, 'Listen, Goardin, Ah've surmezzed that ye've no' been tae the berries afore. Is that richt?'

Gordon nodded, and Brian Turnbull's eyebrows knitted together. 'Ye've done whit, Steevie? Ye've "surnerezzed"?'

Steevie ignored Brian's inquiry and carried on. 'Ye'll mak' fuck all money here unless somebody tells ye how. Seein' it's you, Ah'll gie ye a few wee tricks an' tell ye some o' the rools.'

I could see Gordon's eyes widening as Steevie proceeded to enlighten him with stuff we all knew from experience, and some more besides.

It was just after nine now, and the berry field had been frantic with picking activity for more than an hour. We had arrived late, of course, because we hadn't finished our round till about an hour before, and had been lucky to get a start at all, but still Steevie remained seated.

'First,' said Gordon's new life coach, 'you an' me work as a pair, like on the larry, OK. Every time yer luggie gits full, ye empty it intae oor big pail. Aye?' The pupil nodded his understanding. 'Right. Nivir, ivir let the pail oot o' yer sight. You an' me keep it next tae ane o' us a' day or somebody'll empty it intae theirs. Second, they paiye ye fur the weight o' yer pail, so gie yersel' a wee advantage.'

Gordon looked confused and the rest of us smiled at each other, knowing what advice was coming next.

Steevie took a long drag of his nipper, carefully keeping his fingers away from the tiny glowing shred that remained. 'Piss in it,' he said.

Gordon looked around to check if anybody was laughing and to make sure Steevie wasn't setting him up for a practical joke, but when every one of us greeted his disbelieving look with a resigned shrug, it began to dawn on him that this really was what we did.

'Not too much in one pail, though,' advised Wee Good.

'They ken if it's ower heavy,' Steevie continued Gordon's further education. 'Put the pail atween yer legs a wee bit inside the bushes. Pull yer cock oot an' start peein', but keep baith hands still pickin' so that naebody'll ken ye're addin' a wee drap tae yer earnin's. Dinna worry, it a' gits boiled up in big vats an' a' the gerums gits killed.'

I put a reassuring arm on my Indian friend's broon shoulder. 'A'body diz it, Goardin. In fact, the boy at the weigh-in wid probably wonder how yer pail wiz so light if ye didnae. It's true,' I said, and it was. 'Look aroond in an 'oor or so an' ye'll see them daein' it.'

Steevie moved into advanced instructor mode. 'Third, Goardin, when ye put stanes in yer luggie, mak' sure they're nae bigger than a berry. They can see big rocks, even in among the berries, an' they mak' a clunk when they empty yer pail intae the barrel. They'll run ye aff richt awa' an' no' paiye ye.'

Gordon wandered off to his allotted end of the dreel, his luggie clunking round his thighs, his head filled with newly acquired knowledge, and his professor's big pail in his hand. He must have been wondering if the tea harvesters of India operated a similar system to the berry-pickers of central Scotland.

We worked through the morning as the day grew hotter. All but one of the milk boys were there just for a laugh, and picked at a leisurely pace, only pausing to eat some raspberries and throw a few at the back of each other's heads. Si was the exception. He and his sister were there to make as much money as they could, and picked almost without pause. Si's wee sister picked her twelve-year-old fingers raw, but by half past ten, their big pail was only three-quarters full. Si was working as hard as he could, but he knew it would take them ages to fill it. His wee sister was so intent on her work at the far end of the dreel that she didn't notice Fat Boab reaching through the foliage and emptying half a luggie of berries into her galvanised bucket, so that by eleven o'clock, Si was the first of us to be at the weigh-in cart with their pail collecting his first two shillings and fourpence of the day.

From then on, every time Si's sister tipped a wee hard-earned luggie of raspberries into the huge pail at Si's feet, one of us would sneak our own luggie through the tangle of bushes behind her, and top up her bucket a little bit from our own efforts. Si just smiled and shook his head every time a new hand appeared through the bushes and a few more berries were added. This was the exact opposite of what usually happened when somebody in the next dreel tampered with your pickings.

By twelve o'clock, everybody was sweaty, thirsty and covered in sweet, sticky raspberry juice. It ran down our forearms, dripped off our elbows, covered our hands completely, and slid down our faces where we had wiped the sweat off our foreheads, rubbed our ears or nipped the snot from the end of our noses. God help any boy who succumbed to the temptation to scratch his itchy balls. I'm still convinced that berry juice is Beluga caviar for flies, particularly if it's dripping into the eyes of a boy picker. They were everywhere – up your nose, in your ears, in your hair and around your eyes. Trying to swat them only made things worse, because you always missed the horrible hairy black insect by a whisker, and only succeeded in depositing another dollop of raspberry-flavoured caviar on to your face. Also, raspberry bushes have thorns, and sticking your hands into the middle of the plant to get at the soft fruit inevitably left scratches all over the backs of your hands, or even up your arms if you were daft enough to wear a short-sleeved T-shirt. This must have been fly heaven: sweat, berry juice, fresh urine in many of the pails, followed by a wee bit of bright blood on the backs of a thousand hands for dessert.

The milk crew had been on the go since half past four that morning doing their normal round and were beginning to wilt. Si's sister and my wee brother also had an excuse for feeling tired: they were only twelve and had cycled the seven or eight miles uphill from Dundee to the fields north of Birkhill with the rest of us. Bruce and Brian Turnbull, however, had stayed in bed until half an hour before we set off, so they were insistent that we all pick till one o'clock before we stopped for 'oor dinnur'. At thirty seconds before one, Fat Boab collapsed on the long grass at the edge of the berry field and pulled an emergency bar of McCowan's Highland Toffee from the Red Cross satchel on his hip. He was quickly joined by a berry-covered Wee Good John, Si's sister and Si. Gordon, me and the rest sauntered over to the lee of the drystone dyke beside them, and dumped our haversacks on the grass.

'How much huv ye made, then, Si?' Wee John knew very well that Si and his sister had earned more than any of us, partly because we were pissing about and throwing berries at each other instead of picking to earn money, and partly because a proportion of all our crop was ending up in their pail.

Si's wee sister fairly bubbled out her news. 'We've made fehv an' eight.' She could hardly sit still, and squirmed about looking for approval from her brother's milk-laddie colleagues.

'Fehv an' eight?' I said in mock disbelief. 'That's mair than any o' us. Ye're a demon picker, wee lass. Ye kept that tae yersel'.'

She almost burst with pride for herself and her big brother. 'Ah jist picked the best Ah could.' She beamed.

We sat on the grass beside the stone dyke, swatting flies and opening our lunch bags. The Turnbull twins were obviously dismayed at the amount Si and his sister had earned, and when Steevie, with an innocent look, inquired as to how much money their own morning's effort had produced, Bruce smiled, shook his head and said, 'Four an' ten.' He knew something wasn't right, but he couldn't figure out what it was.

His brother, Brian, was less charitable. 'How did them twa mak' mair than us? That wee lassie could hardly pick her fuckin' nose, nivir mind that much berries.' He waved contemptuously at Si's wee sister sitting smiling on the grass. Her smile vanished and she looked at her brother.

Gordon flashed a warning glance at Brian, and Fat

Boab paused mid-toffee munch. Everybody else's eyes, even Bruce's, darted between Brian and Si.

Si simply patted his sister on the shoulder, and said, 'Brian's only jealous 'cos we've made mair money than him so far, an' he mibbie needs a help tae mak' some fur himsel'.' Then he slowly turned his eyes towards Brian.

When Si got angry or upset, his eyes looked like the aliens on the posters advertising X-rated films outside cinemas. They wouldn't allow us in, of course, because we were under eighteen. It would have been far too traumatic for us to see the Creature From the Arse End of the Universe projecting laser beams from its orange eyes into the forehead of the supporting (expendable) actor, dissolving his brain and causing streams of unconvincing green gunge to ooze from his ears and nose. We were only allowed to watch real blood oozing from the ears and nose of some poor recipient of a good kicking in the street or the pub car park.

Steevie hummed gently to himself, looking down at his right boot, which was involuntarily tapping away on the berry-soaked earth. Gordon was biting his lip, rummaging through his haversack as a displacement activity, but unable to stop himself glancing at Brian every five seconds. The rest of us were avoiding each other's eyes and preparing to move as soon as Si had escorted his sister far enough away from the lesson that Brian Turnbull was about to receive. Even my twelve-year-old brother Ian sensed what was coming.

Si stood up, and Steevie's boots went into double time tapping the soggy earth. Steevie could easily have destroyed Brian and Bruce together on his own, but the rest of the milk crew shifted position to get ready for the inevitable explosion.

Si's benign gaze locked on to Brian Turnbull like an Exocet. 'Wid ye like tae swap wi' me an' pair up wi' ma sister so ye can mak' some real money? Whit d'ye say, Bri? D'ye need a wee hand fae a wee lassie?'

Brian was acutely aware that he'd overstepped the mark and tried to make a dignified retreat. 'Ye ken whit Ah'm sayin', though, Si? This is her first time at the berries an' she's, well, young. Me an' Bruce come here every summer an' we're quick pickers. Ken whit Ah'm sayin'?'

Si grinned broadly. 'Jist eat yer dinnur.'

Peace was restored to the little garden party, and we all delved ravenously into our haversacks. Out came corned-beef rolls, Spam rolls, cheese sandwiches, Tunnock's teacakes, flasks of Mum's thick chicken soup or sweet stewed tea. But when the Turnbull twins pulled several brown-paper bags from a haversack that was once home to a Second World War gas mask and the contents spilled on to the grass, there was a collective moment of disbelief before everybody erupted into fits of choking laughter.

No doubt Mrs Turnbull had considered various options for her sons' luncheon in the berry field – freshly harvested oysters and breast of quail, perhaps, washed down with vintage champagne. She may even have toyed with the idea of including a couple of Cuban cigars for her boys to enjoy before they resumed the afternoon picking session. In the end, though, she had decided on two white rolls spread with Scott's meat paste, and half a Forfar bridie each. So far so good, Mrs Turnbull. It was the other contents of the canvas gas-mask bag that had us all in hysterics. There, amongst the tall grass, wild flowers and bits of brown paper, lay four rolls thickly spread with raspberry jam, along with two pieces of lovingly homemade raspberry crumble and a bottle of fizzy raspberry lemonade.

The guys on the Orange Walk have a representation of a blood-soaked left hand in the middle of their flag, the 'Red Hand of Ulster'. If we had decided to walk on behalf of the 'Noble Order of Berry-Pickers', we would have had twenty berry-juice-soaked hands on our flag, representing all ten of us, the 'Red Hands of Birkhill'. That should give you an idea of how sick we were of raspberries. So who in their right mind would send anybody to the berries with raspberry-jam rolls, raspberry crumble and raspberry lemonade? The last thing in the world that we wanted to consume was anything even remotely tasting of raspberries.

'Serves yez right,' said Wee Good John, grinning from ear to ear. 'Yez should hae got up an' made it yersel's instead o' leavin' it tae yer mum.'

We returned to our berry-picking, and worked in silence for another couple of hours.

We left the field about half past three, partly because the milk laddies were getting bored and tired, but mostly because Wee Good got stung on the back of his neck by a wasp and wasn't having fun any more. As we unchained our bikes and prepared to leave the field, I saw Steevie 'accidentally' fall over Brian's bike so that they were momentarily isolated from the rest of the group. I was too far away to hear what Steevie whispered, but Brian never looked at Si or his sister all the way home.

It's almost all downhill from Birkhill back to Dundee, so we fairly flew home on our assortment of bicycles. Si and his sister were weighed down by the money they'd earned, which increased their downhill velocity, while the Turnbulls were so full of raspberry gas that they almost floated backwards up the hill.

'So are we goin' back the moarn, lads?' said Si, when we reached civilisation and the safety of Kirkton.

'Nae chance,' was Fat Boab's instant reply. 'Ah'm totally knackered. That's worse than doin' the mulk.'

'Me neither,' said Wee Good. 'Ah'm keepin' ma neck well awa' fae they country things.'

Most of the milk laddies made similar decisions.

Steevie could make more money concentrating on his other enterprises, and Gordon and me preferred sitting on the side of the Kingsway harvesting peas. After all, we worked hard enough every morning, and didn't need the money, anyway.

Only the Turnbull twins and Si's wee sister wanted to go back the next day: the Turnbulls because it was their only source of income, and Si's wee sister because she thought berry-picking was dead easy. She had amassed more money than she had ever had, and was ecstatic that her and Si's earnings had beaten every other pair in the whole berry field.

If she and her brother had gone back to the berry fields the next day, though, their wages would have more than halved, no matter how much Si pissed into the pail, and everybody except her and the Turnbull brothers knew why. Si managed to convince his sister that he was so tired out he risked sleeping in for his round the following morning, so he couldn't take her again. She was badly disappointed, of course, but her brother's excuse wasn't a million miles from the truth for all of Avril's milk-laddie berry-pickers.

Chapter Seven

I Laid Up Treasure

'He who lays up treasure for himself and is
not rich towards God . . .'
Luke, 12:21

In 1962, a pound a week was five times what a paperboy got and nearly a quarter of the wages of a first-year apprentice car mechanic. When tips of between seventeen and twenty-four shillings were added on top, milk laddies were earning a fortune. We talked about 'makin' a Klon', by which we meant that we had struck as rich a seam of gold as some of the luckiest prospectors in the Klondike, who toiled in mines and icy streams to eventually become dollar millionaires. We knew that we were being exploited, but we didn't care, because we were earning so much money we could live like rock stars.

I told my mum that I was earning eighteen shillings a week and getting about six shillings in tips. She thought for a few seconds, trying not to look too shocked at the enormity of the sum, before announcing that half my wages was a reasonable contribution to the house, but she would let me keep the other half of my pay and all my tips if I gave some of it towards an investment for my future. 'This is a whole lot o' money fur ye, Wullie, mair than me or yer faither ivir hud at your age,' she said gravely. 'So if ye want tae gie me some o' yer extra money, Ah'll open a bank accoont fur ye an' ye can start savin' up fur yer feutchir.'

I didn't give a toss for my 'feutchir', but I knew it would make life easier if I complied, so I put on my responsible look and offered a shilling a week.

'Weel, that's no' very much aff a' that money ye'll hae left, son,' she said in her best bank manager's voice. 'How aboot half a croon a week? That'll gie ye ten bob in yer accoont every single month an' ye'll still hae elivin shillin's tae yersel'.'

I tried to look pained. 'If ye think it's in ma best intrists, Ma. You ken best.'

This still left me upwards of twenty-two shillings every week to spend on nothing but myself, an unbelievable sum that had grown to nearly thirty bob by the end of my first year, when I was better known to my regulars and my tip-maximisation techniques had been honed to perfection. But it got even better. At the beginning of the Dundee summer-holiday fortnight, almost every worker in the town had collected holiday pay or bonuses or both, and was intoxicated by the heady power of having limitless amounts of ready cash. The pubs were full of men trying to buy each other drinks, and the bookies swarmed with punters, spilling out over the pavement and offering each other cigarettes.

This was as bountiful a harvest as any milk laddie could hope for and we 'milked' it to the last.

'Whit a luv'ly day, Mrs Shultz. Mulk money, please.'

'Aye, eet iz nice tae see the sun. Oh! an' we'll no' be needin' ony mulk till next Seturday.'

'OK, consider that done, missus. So are ye goin' awa' fur yer holidays, then?'

'Aye, a hale week in Butlin's.'

'That must be brilliant . . . Me?' I managed to look as if I was dejected but bearing up stoically. 'Nae, Ah'm no' goin' awa' this year. Ma dad's been put on shoart time at the shipyaird.'

And so it went on from door to door, every conversation a variation on the same theme until they said the blessed words 'There ye go, Wullie, there's a wee somethin' fur yer holidays.' On the last Friday before the July 1963 Dundee trades fortnight, I came home with a pound in wages and nearly five pounds ten in tips. I felt light-headed.

Christmas tips were nearly as good as the summer-holiday tips, although some women in the posh houses gave us little bags of cake or nuts. That was OK, but not nearly as OK as cash. New Year's tips were a washout, though, because every household was broke, having overdone the hospitality and the bevvy. So they either gave us a big embarrassed smile and no money, or occasionally a bit of shortbread or a 'wee warm toddy tae keep oot the cauld'. Once again I came home light-headed.

During normal weeks, people gave us tips of pennies, thruppenny bits and occasionally even tanners. If a house got two pints a day, the weekly bill came to nine shillings and fourpence, so 'Mulk money, please' would usually elicit a ten-bob note. The eightpence change therefore had to be given to the customer in a mixture of coins, thus providing several permutations of tip. If the house only got a pint a day delivered, then the bill at the end of the week was just four shillings and eightpence, which gave the customer a lot less leeway, so the only possibilities were 'There's thruppence fur ye, Wullie', 'Keep the twa pennies, son', 'Tak' a penny yersel', lad', or the dreaded 'Thank ye very much. See ye next week.'

The exception was Pat O'Rafferty, who was the best tipper on my round and gave me a whole shilling to myself every week when I collected his milk money. He lived in a stone bungalow with a slate roof and dormer windows that must have once been a rural 'des-res', nestling in a picturesque orchard beside the old country road to the village of Glamis, where the Queen Mother spent her childhood, but which soon degenerated into a dilapidated heap after it was swallowed by the sprawling Kirkton housing estate. The previous owners had tried to defend their Alamo against the rushing onslaught of the massed lower orders by building a six-foot-high brick wall round the entire property. It wasn't so much a garden wall as a fortification that the Knights Templar would have been proud of, and it completely enclosed the house's quarter-acre grounds. Although their wall surely bled them of their lifetime's savings, it held back the waves of Dundee's rehoused proletariat as ineffectively as King Cnut's bellowed commands stopped the incoming tide, so Cnut ended up with his knees covered in cold saltwater, while Mr and Mrs Middle Class sold up to Mr O'Rafferty at a huge loss and moved out.

The newly built council houses on the northern periphery of Kirkton lapped against the southern redoubt of Mr and Mrs Middle Class's now-decaying idyllic cottage home, and the yard where plum trees once dropped their ripe fruit on to clipped green lawns was now home to a litter of scrap cars, motorbike engines, rusty bikes, rats and other assorted goodies. Pat had improved the defences with cemented-in broken glass and coils of barbed wire on top of the walls, and a couple of muscular black dogs that frothed and slavered around the dead vans strewn between heaps of rusty twisted metal stuff.

These canine nightmares were designed for one purpose only: killing. Their brains were hot-wired to kill anything that was warm, from a tadpole to a woolly mammoth, and they were perfectly capable of ripping an adult human apart in less than 2.4 seconds. An adolescent milk laddie may have taken a half-second less, but the result would have been the same.

Every morning near the end of my round, I found myself gazing nervously into the eyes of two of these aberrations. The dogs' eyes burned with the beautiful coldness of every ruthless predator on the planet, and I avoided meeting these eyes for the same reason that I avoided the eyes of some of the boys in Kirkton: they shared the same wiring diagram.

I never did find out what Pat actually did in his yard, but every time I arrived at the big iron gate he was always engrossed in doing it, making showers of sparks soar above blinding blue-white light with his scary welding mask and his oxy-acetylene thingy. He always looked as if he'd been working since I started my round for some reason, so we both must have been on the go for about four hours before the cops started the dayshift. I suspected that he welded bits of written-off vans, discarded prams and abandoned wheelchairs together to form completely roadworthy motor vehicles, available at never-to-be-beaten special offers, but I didn't like to ask.

Pat was from Northern Ireland and was my best customer. I delivered his pint of milk every morning on the last stop before the lorry arrived back at the depot, and he always paused in his remodelling work to come and get the bottle from me just inside the gate. I think this was probably because he didn't want to have to take time out from welding to explain to the police about the disappearance of a local milk laddie while his dogs lay contentedly licking their lips inside a collapsed and bloodstained Austin A40. He always took a couple of minutes to chat as we exchanged a full bottle for an empty, or when he pressed the milk money and extravagant tip into my hand on a Friday night. Gradually, Pat and I became good pals.

Here lay the root of the one problem in our relationship. Normally, chats between chums need each chum to understand the language used by the other chum. In the case of Pat and me, I hardly understood a tenth of what he was saying, and I usually just nodded and grinned and said, 'Oh, aye, Pat, ye're right enough,' every time there was a break in his flow. I think he thought I was simple, which maybe explained the big tip. A thick Belfast accent is a bit difficult to keep up with at the best of times, unlike a thick Dundee accent, which can be readily understood by everyone ('Eh skelt meh pehs doon the loaby, an' a' meh pehs went skeh heh'), but Pat had another couple of barriers to communication in his repertoire: he talked at ninety-four miles an hour, at ninety-five decibels, and he inserted 'fuck', or, as he pronounced it, 'fock', between every second word. He would even insert 'fock' in the middle of words with more than three syllables, producing descriptive new adjectives like 'Joi-fockin'-gantic', and nouns that were eleven inches long like the Germans have: 'Duffur-fockin'-enshill-fockin'-ovurhead-dustrubutur-fockin'-cap'. All I could make out of our little morning heart-to-hearts was that several things in his life were 'oit-fockin'-raaayjos' and that several other things were a 'daia-fockin'-bollicull-fockin'-liburtae'.

As the weeks went past, I began to think of my customers as 'tippers' rather than people. Mrs Barry and her three young children became 'Barry – two pints a day and a one-penny tipper', while the 50-odd per cent of customers who were non-tippers just faded into the obscurity of how many milk bottles I had to leave on their doorstep. I even began to subconsciously value my pal Pat's shiny shilling tip more than our amusing 'convur-fockin'-sayshuns'.

Slowly, imperceptibly, by little inches Gordon and me changed. I suppose we were afflicted by the syndrome that overcomes many present-day lottery winners: the creeping, mind-altering opiate of wealth that whispers the poor addict further and further away from reality. We each had more money at our disposal than half of our classmates could muster between them, but we didn't realise how much we were flaunting our wealth.

The real truth was, no matter how much Auld Jim paid us (which wasn't all that much, really), we were becoming weary running about in the cold, damp mornings. We needed a break from front-line combat and a bit of R&R. So one Saturday morning, out of the blue, Wee Good John suggested that we all go to the 'sweemin' pool' in the afternoon. This was astonishing since Wee Good was the least athletic person on the planet, and should have been the last to come up with a suggestion like that.

'Let's do it,' I said, and two minutes later it was all arranged.

Dundee Corporation's Swimming Baths were opened in a triumph of uniformed brass bands and union flags somewhere around the middle of Queen Victoria's reign. Several Dundee 'toon coonsellors' in tail coats and top hats claimed personal credit for bringing this wonderful public work to the city in speeches delivered to a handful of shivering citizens, horses and press reporters huddled in the cold, damp mist that drifts out of the North Sea over the Dundee docks. No wonder Captain Scott decided to piss off to the South Pole in his *Discovery*.

Our sweemin'-pool building was identical to the

municipal bathing facilities constructed in Forfar, Colchester, Rangoon, Cape Town and everywhere else where we still mattered. Bands probably played the same tunes at the opening of British Empire public baths around the world, and the same wee local gold-chained official would make the same wee speech: 'As your elected representative on the municipal council for —, it gives me enormous personal pleasure . . .' Aye, right, pal. The designers of these edifices firmly believed that the whole world would eventually be encrusted in wrought iron and glass, so huge structures were commissioned, covering everything from railway stations to museums, botanical gardens and swimming pools. Victorian politicians believed that acres of glass and white tiles, combined with unlimited supplies of hot water would keep the masses clean, healthy, amused and under control.

The Corporation baths consisted of several distinct areas. The most ornate section was the 'big pool', where ladies and gentlemen bathed together under a viewing gallery and a vast umbrella of glass and elegant white-painted rivets. Little wooden cubicles up each side of the pool provided customers with primitive changing facilities, and patrons were issued with a coloured wrist band when they handed over their clothes, safe in a wee wire basket to be stored in the racks behind the attendants' counter. The water was three times saltier than the Dead Sea, and the level of chlorine would today be considered a war crime. A diving board at the deep end rose about twelve feet above the water's surface, and lines of young boys took it in turns to 'depth-charge' elderly women swimmers. This move consisted of leaping from the board, curling into a ball, and landing as close to the woman as possible. It was particularly gratifying if she was wearing one of these bathing caps with artificial flowers all over it, because she and her cap would be swamped under a tidal wave. When Fat Boab depth-charged, it was like a mini tsunami and a wall of water covered everybody in the top half of the pool.

Ladies had a pool of their own somewhere at the far end of the building where we never went. There were also Turkish baths, saunas and porcelain tubs for people who still lived in the old tenements with outside toilets. We never went near these facilities in the building either, since some of the men who patronised them looked distinctly wild, or drunk, or smiled at us, or were plainly in need of a wash.

The pool we used most was the 'wee pool'. It was only for men and boys, and was permanent bedlam. Hundreds of little pale stick insects thrashed about in every square inch of surface water, so the pool frothed and boiled like the upper reaches of the Amazon after a shoal of piranha have caught a calf in mid-stream. The screams of little boys shouting, laughing, trying to learn to swim over the top of each other, punching and urinating into the water echoed off the wrought-iron rafters all day.

Some boys brought their own swimming trunks, some wore trunks hired from Dundee Corporation, which hung down around their thighs like wet dish towels, and some didn't bother to replace these soggy articles when they inevitably fell off completely. To cap it all, when the 'man' went away for a cup of tea or a smoke, several boys would climb on to the top of the doorless changing cubicles and leap out into the pool. During attendant smoking breaks, you were in grave danger of being smacked in the head by a naked stick insect leaping from the top of a changing cubicle right above you.

The wee pool had no showers, but it did have an enormous porcelain bath that you were supposed to wash your feet in before going in the pool. This was fine in principle, except that the bath was invariably filled by an older fat lad wallowing in the hot water. Of course, on the day that we chose to go swimming, as usual a teenage Godfather was enjoying the warmth of the bath for himself, while half-a-dozen cold, nervous little boys stood around. Steevie went up to the bath and tried to dip his foot around Don Corleone's shoulder, provoking the response 'Git that foot the fuck oot o' ma bath.'

'So sorry, pal,' says Steevie humbly, and took his foot out of the tub.

The guy's soft face looked quite smug for a few seconds as he settled back into the hot water, until a foot wiped over his mouth and chin. He spat into the bath and cast a disbelieving glance at Steevie. 'Ye wee bastard,' he roared, putting both his hands on the sides of the bath. When he was halfway up, Steevie hit him in the temple just above his left ear and the guy dropped like a rock, flopping half his fat-arsed body out of the bath. The crowd of little boys fell on him like a pack of hyenas and gleefully stamped all over his body on the tiled floor. Steevie calmly washed his feet in the bath as the pool regulations required.

For the next hour, we jumped about in the salty water, practising our Olympic record-breaking freestyle technique and avoiding airborne white stick insects, while the 'Knight of the Bath' was carted away, semiconscious and dripping blood from his nose over the floor.

Sadly, the arrogance of wealth started right from my first pay packet. Gordon, Fat Boab and me went into town on Saturday afternoon and wandered about knowing that we could buy almost anything we liked. As soon as we were off the bus, Boab bought a footlong Toblerone and we headed towards the Mecca of every model-railway enthusiast and construction-kit builder in the city. Brian Shepherd's was a shop that specialised in model-making, and it was an Aladdin's cave of treasure for every boy from seven to seventy.

Ranks of soldiers, train sets, racing cars, tanks, aircraft and warships lined the shelves, and little Spitfires and Messerschmitts hung by invisible threads from a sky-blue ceiling, frozen in a never-ending dogfight. The walls and counters were jammed full of plastic construction kits in huge boxes covered in stunning artwork, depicting the model inside releasing a stack of bombs over a blazing target or belching flames from fifteen-inch guns as it engaged a distant enemy.

I had twenty-one shillings in my pocket, which, apart from complete train sets or the lacquered teak model yachts that the grown-up men bought, could buy almost any of the shiny jewels that Brian Shepherd was offering. My mind began to whirl at the thought of what I could have, and, even more startling, what Gordon and me could accomplish between us. 'We could build a whole skwadrin o' Spitfiers, Goardin.'

Gordon and me stared at the rows of little cellophane packets containing 1:72 scale-model Supermarine Spitfires and Hawker Hurricanes, knowing that we could buy the lot. Every boy in Britain had spent at least a week's pocket money on the little Airfix model Spitfire in his bedroom, but we could have an airfield's worth and still have money to spare.

'They're one an' six each,' I said. 'If you wiz tae get ten, that wid be fifteen bob, an' if Ah wiz tae get anithir ten, that wid gie us twenty fighters, an' we'd still hae enough money fur the gloo an' the pent an' loads tae spare.'

Fat Boab looked around blankly, presumably checking out if the shop stocked any plastic confectionery or model-pie kits.

'We could set up an assem'ly line like they done in the waar,' said Gordon, who was becoming as enthusiastic as me now. 'You could pent the pilots an' Ah'll pent the inside o' the cockpits. Then Ah'll stick the feooziladgis thegither an' you could gloo on the weengs.'

We were on the verge of commissioning our first fighter squadron when the striking vision of an American battleship struggling through mountainous seas powered majestically out at Gordon from high up on a shelf devoted to the more discerning practitioner of the plastic-model-builder's craft. The painting was on the lid of a construction kit made by a company called Revell, who we had never heard of before; after all, a one an'-six Airfix Fockurwoolf' was as much as we could previously aspire to.

Suddenly, Gordon whistled through his teeth and looked up from his cellophane-packaged fledgling Spitfire squadron. 'Look at that, Wullie – is that no' the fuckin' berries?' and right away I knew that the air force would have to take care of itself, because my best friend and me were destined to become scale-model admirals.

USS *North Carolina* cost all of seventeen and six, but she was magnificent. At nearly two feet long, she was the biggest and most breathtaking plastic model I'd ever seen, and I knew in an instant that I just had to have her. 'Nivir mind a skwadrin, Goardin – let's build a great big huge fleet.' So I bought this leviathan and cradled her in my arms all the way home on the back seat of the Kirkton bus. Gordon contributed Airfix's version of the battlecruiser HMS *Hood* to the fleet, and he also bought all the 'gloo an' pent' we would need. The fact that the real HMS *Hood* and USS *North Carolina* never came within ten thousand miles of each other didn't occur to us: Gordon and me were about to build the most powerful navy the world had known. Fat Boab sat between us on the back seat and devoured the last triangle of his Swiss confection, but I quietly gloated in the knowledge that my USS *North Carolina* was three times as big as any Toblerone.

For the next three or four months, Gordon and me laboured tirelessly to produce a mighty naval taskforce of Revell battleships, Frogg aircraft carriers and Airfix cruisers, destroyers and landing craft. We spent endless hours together up in my bedroom, fiddling with tiny little anti-aircraft guns and searchlights so they would fit perfectly into their deck-mounted housings, or painting detailed camouflage patterns on miniature torpedo bombers for the decks of the aircraft carriers. Every week's tips launched a new wave of naval craft on to my bedroom carpet until you couldn't see the floor for swarms of grey plastic warships, each separated from its out-of-scale neighbour by at least eighteen nautical inches of polyester.

Eventually, we had everything necessary to overwhelm any country anywhere. At our whim, two British and six American aircraft carriers, supported by eight great battleships, could launch hundreds of little planes against any target that took our fancy. This awesome strike force was protected by dozens of cruisers and destroyers, and the whole fleet was supported by two tankers and a white-painted hospital ship with big red crosses on the sides. This was more than Admiral Nagumo needed to destroy Pearl Harbor.

Slowly, Gordon and me began to display all the arrogance of superpowers throughout history: 'We've got loads of money and a huge military capability, so we're much better than the rest of you.' Every Saturday Brian Shepherd's shop was filled with boys spending all their pocket money on a little plastic tank or a one-and-six Spitfire, and I began to derive warped pleasure in being able to swagger through the throng and lay a nineteen-shilling model of some USS *Enormous* in front of the till.

But the bigger our fleet became, the smaller buzz we got from the launch of each new ship. We began to compromise on the perfect positioning of every searchlight and life raft, until some of the ships we were finally sending to the fleet were distinctly uncarpetworthy. We tried hard to disguise our boredom from each other by creating ever more ridiculous missions for our unstoppable naval force, like setting out hundreds of matches that were really junks full of Imperial Chinese Commie infantry bent on invading Carnoustie, or positioning Gordon's dad's scary stuffed crocodile thing in the middle of my bedroom, recreated as the Creature From the Lost Lagoon, so it could be pounded to death by our guns and planes. In every scenario, our fleet utterly destroyed whatever it was sent against, until there was no excitement being an invincible plastic admiral any more.

Adding to the fleet got to be the same as learning your milk round: a mechanical thing that had to be done, but only while you were thinking of something else. Learning your milk round was like spouting out your times tables when you were at primary school: 'Seven sixes are forty-two. Seven sevens are forty-nine.' Most young boys' minds were a thousand miles away, firing Winchester rifles at cattle rustlers and saving the herd for Chuckie, Ole Doc McLeod, Scalp-'Em-at-Bedtime (the token red Indian on our side) and Flint McClintock (the handsome leader of the wagon train), while the girls in our class were chanting the same tables as us, except they were far away giving flawless performances of the Highland Fling in front of Her Majesty the Queen, His Majesty Cliff Richard, their tearfully emotional mum and grannie, and a less than majestic dotty old auntie Aggie, all magically transported to the grand banqueting hall of Balmoral Castle for the occasion.

The same robotic learning processes were at work with us milk laddies as we committed the round to memory: Shepherd – twa pints. Lawrence – ane pint an' twa on Seturday. Rafferty – three pints. Buchan – ane pint. Then a wee pause, a deep breath: Nearly there, Wullie. Only ane pint fur Mrs Unpronounceable Russian Name That Looks Like a Bad Scrabble Hand. Then there was only my fockin' good unin-fockin'-tellegable mate Pat to go and I would be finished.

Like the times tables, the milk round was mechanically burned into our minds so that it was always just below the surface, no matter how much Grand Admiral Lord Gordon of Kirkton and First Sea Lord Willie developed their maritime power. So it didn't come as a surprise when Gordon suddenly mused, after delivering another three newly painted tiny Swordfish torpedo bombers to the flight deck of HMS *Victorious* one afternoon, 'Whar d'ye think the crates o' milk comes fae, Wullie?'

Well, this was too daft to be true, so I looked as serious as I could, thought for a few moments and said, 'Ah think they probably come fae cows, Goardin.'

I was kneeling on the floor, concentrating on providing USS *Tuscaloosa* with a little accurate seaplane to fit on the launching ramp at her stern when a sharp skelp on the back of my head projected my face into the back half of the cruiser, causing more damage than a squadron of kamikazes. Seconds later, my head was being painfully twisted against Gordon's chest as his forearm tightened round my throat in a head grip, restricting my breathing. Gordon's arms were strong, and I was seeing lovely orange flashes at the back of my eyes. The cruiser's wee camouflaged seaplane whirled off through the clear blue South Pacific sky towards the wardrobe, and I squirmed my head backwards to try to suck in more air, while my right hand instinctively moved to Gordon's balls. There's no more eloquently persuasive argument in the whole world than a hand slowly crushing one's testicles.

Gordon's voice squealed higher and higher, 'OK, Wullie, OK, OK, OKAAAYY!' and he speedily relinquished his hold round my neck, but then ignominiously broke the terms of the Geneva Convention and his unconditional surrender by playfully smacking me a bit too hard round the head as soon as my hand let go of his tender bits. 'Ye ken whit Ah mean, though? How diz a' they galluns o' milk get there every single moarnin'?' He looked quite wistful, gazing, misty-eyed, into the semi-distance, rubbing his squashed bollocks, and maybe remembering his childhood in India and the wonders of how such a vast multitude could be kept in rice every day. Or maybe he was just thinking about how the population of Dundee could be kept in milk.

To be truthful, it had occasionally crossed my mind how so many stacks of full milk crates could be waiting for us every morning without fail when the laddies turned up at around ten to five. Somebody must be organising this as well as providing the logistical support to make it all possible. Although it never kept me awake at night, Gordon's question articulated my own thoughts and aroused my simple curiosity. How did thousands of gallons of milk materialise every morning at the depot?

I briefly considered dispatching the entire USS *Enterprise* battle group (three carriers, four battleships and a dozen support vessels, including the cruiser *Tuscaloosa* and her wee seaplane) to get to the bottom of the question, but decided on the less expensive option. 'We'll ask Avril the moarn.'

'It comes fae the DPM in Strathmartine Road, Wullie,' Avril said absently in response to my question, wincing at the way her dad's face contorted as he pulled his old body up into the cab for yet another morning. 'That stands fur "Dundee Pashchoorezed Mulk". Ah think it wiz set up durin' the First Wurld Waar,' she said to no one.

That didn't help Gordon or me one bit. 'Whit is this DPM, though, Avril?'

Everybody knew the big wide entrance wedged between the endless line of tenement flats in Strathmartine Road, with the words 'DPM' etched in the stone lintel as confidently as any 'SPQR' above an archway in Rome. Nobody knew where the entrance led, though, and very few knew that DPM stood for 'Dundee Pashchoorezed Mulk'. The vast majority of Dundonians would probably have accepted the explanation that it stood for 'Dundonium Pasturisium Milkius' as an attempt by Edwardian stonemasons to recreate imperial glory.

Anyway, it seemed that the lorries from the outlying dairy farms brought their produce to the DPM every afternoon, where it was pasteurised and bottled and stored in giant coldrooms. Avril and Auld Jim picked up their quota every morning at four o'clock, so that it could be back in the depot when we all arrived.

Next day, Gordon and me didn't contribute anything to the fleet. We didn't even invade Russia. We just sat looking at the fruits of all our months of labour, thinking of Avril and her dad reversing the lorry under the carved letters 'DPM' at five to four every morning. Our mighty fleet suddenly seemed trivial, and for the first time I saw it for what it really was: a carpet covered in wee toys.

To cap it all, my mum was becoming mightily disappointed with my obsession for building model ships when I should have been obsessed with doing homework, and I could tell that she was also getting increasingly unimpressed as every flat surface and storage shelf in my bedroom slowly filled up with warships. 'Ye'll be fine if ye get a question in yer O level aboot plastic boats' and 'This bookcase wiz suppost tae be fur yer skaelbooks, no' fur wee toys.' Even when we covered HMS *Cossack* with lighter fluid and set fire to her in a bath full of water, all we got out of it was a bathroom filled with acrid smoke, a sticky black woodchip ceiling and my mum's hysterical ranting for nearly twenty minutes.

We were saying goodbye to our childhood, and just like Puff the Magic Dragon, painted wings and giant rings were making way for other toys. Our painted destroyers and giant battleships were about to be swept aside by unexpected 'toys' that would have more impact on our lives than we could ever imagine. When these toys arrived one dark, cold night in the middle of October 1962, they hit us out of nowhere with inconceivable force and life-altering consequences.

Chapter Eight

'Love Me Do'

The three little words that changed so much.

I never liked fairgrounds or carnivals – probably because I couldn't see the point of giving your money to some oily-haired gypsy so you could be thrown about in a gaudily painted crate for three minutes – but Gordon and me were moving on from our painted wings and plastic boats: we needed another distraction and somewhere to spend our money. When a carnival arrived in town, every teenager who was halfway cool had to show their face, so me and Gordon, Fat Boab and eight or nine of our other mates leaned against the rail of the waltzers one evening in mid-October 1962, trying to see up the skirt of any girl who got caught in the slipstream, and listening to the Shadows' latest record being played too loudly over the tinny loudspeakers.

As usual, Si wasn't with us because he was looking after his wee sister while his mum sliced bacon in the Co-op. Steevie was absent because his uncle Stuart had committed hara-kiri in the Albert Bar the night before: ritual suicide by filling one's honourable intestines with vodka and Irn-Bru.

Suddenly, a bolt of primal energy erupted from the speakers surrounding the squelchy ash-and-cinders car park that was Dundee's temporary Las Vegas. As one, our little team slowly stood upright as the sound assaulted our very being. All around us boys and girls decelerated dodgem cars, lowered air rifles with doctored sights or just stared at each other like zombies in a B-movie.

Gordon took two paces forward into the glare of a thousand coloured light bulbs and stared at the speakers with his mouth half open; even Fat Boab's brilliantly polished Protestant shoes were beating time in the damp gravel as he stood transfixed with candy floss hanging from his lips. It was a sound like nothing we'd ever heard before. It was raw, vibrant, thumping, rebellious and real, and this new dimension in music didn't just come in through your ears; it invaded your whole body via every nerve ending. A throaty harmonica and tribal drumbeat sounded the opening strains of the most electric sound I'd ever known, and then a harmony of voices filled the makeshift stadium with 'Love Me Do'. I went as weak at the knees as any Victorian virgin after her first kiss. Like a rat following the Pied Piper, the world was blotted out and I could only listen, hypnotised, to the record that ushered out my boyhood and welcomed in the beginnings of my life as a young man.

Gordon and me glanced briefly at each other, and in an instant we both knew that the ships of our mighty high-seas fleet were about to be mothballed on top of the wardrobe or scuttled in the depths of the bin at the back door under seventy fathoms of squelchy potato peelings and assorted household gunk. Sure enough, shares in Brian Shepherd's model shop nose-dived the very next Saturday as Gordon, Boab, Steevie and me, along with hundreds of other teenagers in the city, went in search of the sound. We didn't have to search very long, though.

I'd been in a record shop once before, and only then to pretend I had enough money to buy the top-ten hit 'Apache' by the Shadows so I could hear it played in the wee booth. Now, before I got into the shop, I could hear 'Love Me Do' spilling out from several of the booths. Although Johnny and the rest of the street-cred aristocracy were still buying Elvis, Cliff Richard and Patsy Cline, every now and again I could hear a voice at the front of the queue asking for '"Luv Me Do" by the Beatuls, please.' Then it was my turn to add a little pebble to the coming landslide as the late-twenty-something woman behind the counter looked lazily over my right shoulder at some Brylcreemed teddy boy and idly droned, 'Aye, next?'

' "Luv Me Do" by the Beatuls, please,' I said politely.

Unfortunately, I wasn't tall enough, old enough, cool enough or Brylcreemed enough, so all I got in return was the word 'Whit?' shooting past my right ear on the same trajectory as her lecherous stare at the teddy boy.

'"Luv Me Do" by the Beatuls, missus.'

Without a word, she turned to the racks behind her, pulled out a little vinyl record in a green-paper sleeve and placed it on the counter. 'That's six an' eight,' she said, to my left ear this time because her teddy-boy fantasy had moved a couple of feet, so I put two half-crowns and a two-shilling coin on the counter while she slipped the record into a paper bag. The whole transaction had taken place without us ever actually making eye contact, and I just made out 'Aye, next' as I walked away from the counter with fourpence change and my precious cargo.

The bus home seemed to travel at half its usual speed, and at every stop some old woman took ten minutes getting off or a young mother needed help with a pram and fifty bags of messages. Eventually, we made it to my house and the four of us hunched around my dad's radiogram.

The little green-paper sleeve had the word 'Parlophone' written over it, and it had a hole in the middle round which you could read the words 'Love Me Do' and 'The Beatles'. The middle of the record also had the words '45 rpm' on it, so I flicked the radiogram switch from the thirty-three setting for my dad's LPs to the forty-five setting for my one and only record, then reverently slid the black vinyl out of its protective cover.

The mystical moment was ruined, though, when Gordon said, 'How come it's forty-fehv revulooshuns a meenit? How is it no' twenty-nine, or a hundred an' sixty-two? Who invented a' this?'

Steevie chirped up, true to form, 'Who gives a fuck? Jist pit the record on, Wullie.'

Boab shook his head and absently sucked his Caramac bar.

'Dinna you swear in the hoose, Steevie,' I snapped. 'Ma mum'll hae ye oot o' here in half a tick.'

'Sorry, Wullie, Ah wisnae thinkin'. Ah didnae mean—'

'Aye, well, think next time or Ah'll pit ye oot masel'.'

'Oh, fur Christ's sake, you twa— Oh, sorry, Wullie.' Gordon looked at the floor and blushed.

I could feel myself getting angry and heated, climbing up to the moral high ground, but before I was halfway up the slope, Fat Boab, having dealt with his Caramac, magically produced a bar of McCowan's Highland Toffee from the unplumbed depths of his trouser pocket. His skilled hands expertly broke the bar into eight equal segments and he silently laid a single segment in front of Gordon, Steevie and me with the precision of a priest dispensing bread at communion. The remaining five segments went in front of himself, but the gesture had been made and the god of gluttony had been appeased by his supreme sacrifice. Through this one stupid act, Boab turned the whole tense moment into a big joke and within moments I was sliding the record down the spike and on to the turntable. In the few short seconds before needle touched vinyl and the Beatles filled the room with their unforgettable sound, the only noise was the quiet hiss of the turntable and Fat Boab gently sucking his Highland Toffee.

Then whack! it was as if somebody had slapped me in the lug.

Even at the first note my body shuddered, and my brain reeled under the blitzkrieg of drums and harmonica. When the voices began, all my senses went haywire and I felt a physical reaction in my head, my stomach and my balls. I didn't know that sound could do this to people. I felt vital, alive and filled with limitless energy, and I could see that this music was having the same effect on the rest of the lads. Gordon and Steevie just stared at the laminated teak-effect radiogram, while Boab's jaws attacked the four squares of Highland Toffee in his mouth like a high-performance pneumatic drill. The sound of the three magic words 'love me do' reverberated through our bodies and the whole room pulsated with a raw, rebellious energy that could have been measured on the Richter scale.

'WHIT THE BLOODY HELL'S GOIN' ON HERE?' Obviously my mum was impervious to the musical spell and could look Medusa straight in the face. In fact, when my mum was in this kind of mood, her stare would have turned the Gorgon to stone. 'WULLIE! Turn that bloody racket doon right now.'

So much for my moral high ground and not swearing in the house.

But the conversion was complete, and Gordon and me had become devoted Beatle disciples. We played that record every moment when we had the living room and my dad's radiogram to ourselves. It was quickly obvious, though, that we couldn't carry on sneaking in the Beatles in the spare moments when my mum and dad weren't cooing over Nat King Cole or the soundtrack from *Oklahoma!*: it wasn't nearly rebellious enough. We had to get a record player of our own.

There must have been an emergency meeting in Brian Shepherd's boardroom when they heard that

Gordon and me were going to spend almost all of our combined week's wages and tips on a record player, and not even fourpence on a little tin of battleship-grey 'pent'. The following Saturday afternoon, the two of us clubbed together and bought the best record player in the shop. It was a two-tone grey plastic box with a lid that opened to reveal a turntable, switches and an arm with an upmarket diamond needle at the end. The guy wasn't overly impressed when we paid in pennies, thruppennies, tanners and shilling coins, but he filled his till to overflowing and we left with the very latest that electronic technology and plastic injection moulding could produce.

All the rest of that afternoon and evening we sat in raptures listening to 'Love Me Do', then turned it over and listened to 'PS I Love You', then turned it over and listened to 'Love Me Do' again. Nobody ever got more money's worth out of any product than me and Gordon got from our little plastic record player and our one wee record. We played it over and over until the upmarket diamond needle scraped halfway through the vinyl and the three-pin plug got dangerously hot. We played it all through November and December, and even listened out for when they played it on the radio. We memorised all the words and rehearsed all the harmonies, and I even dug out my dad's rusty old mouth organ so I could attempt the harmonica bits. Mind you, it didn't sound quite as raunchy on an instrument that was used to belting out 'Ye Canna Shove Yer Grannie Aff a Bus' at Hogmanay, but it was near enough for us at the time. I've still got that very same record in its little green-paper sleeve. It's probably worth a few quid now to some collector, but to me it's priceless.

Just after we came back from the Christmas holiday, a huge buzz went round the school. The word was that the Beatles were going to release another record called 'Please Please Me' that month, and everybody wanted to be among the first to hear it, and even better, among the first to tell everybody else that they'd heard it. Sure enough, one morning, about ten people announced to the class that they'd heard 'Please Please Me' on some radio programme and that it was 'oot o' this wurld'. Even people who hadn't actually heard the record but wanted a claim to fame swore it was 'jist too much fur me tae discribe'. Of course, Gordon and me had been too busy collecting milk money to hear the inaugural playing, so the two of us had to join the crowd of 'non-hearers' listening to the ravings of the privileged few.

OK, maybe we hadn't heard it, but we could buy it and most of the rest couldn't. Only the ones who hadn't spent their Christmas money from Auntie Betty could afford to go out and blow nearly seven shillings in one go. The non-milk-deliverers had to save up for about four weeks or beg their mum for a handout, but

Gordon and me had doubled our record collection by the next Friday night without a thought for the massive expense.

We flaunted our wealth shamelessly, like we were characters in some black-and-white B-movie about teenage Sicilian hoods in New York's Lower East Side, and we bought everything we could get our hands on to reinforce our status. When the Beatles were photographed wearing Cuban-heeled boots, Gordon and me were out the next day to get a pair. Even Fat Boab bought a pair, although he looked like a hippo on stilts when he tried them on. 'Ye'll no' get allowed tae wear them on yer Oringe Walk, Boab. Fowk'll think ye're a wee fat Prodistint poof.' Even if he did look like a wee fat Prodistint poof, the three of us were becoming recognised in the playground as 'hip' and 'groovy'. Our hair had grown over our ears and we strutted about in our high-heeled boots trying to talk like John Lennon or Mick Jagger, although Wee Good still looked like a poor wee soul whatever he wore, and Steevie was much too busy expanding his recycled tobacco business to care about hip or groovy: he just wanted the money.

My dad was the foreman in a joiner's shop. He kept about twenty men under control through a blend of diplomacy and quiet authority, and if there was a non-confrontational route to anywhere, my dad would find it. In fact, if he'd been born in Kensington, he would have made an excellent diplomat in some forgotten outpost of our shrinking empire. If my mum had joined Her Majesty's Diplomatic Service, though, we would have been at war with every country on the planet within two months. Her Irish ancestry always boiled just below the surface, and her heart completely ruled her head. No wonder my dad wanted to marry her.

If my mum was happy, we knew it. If she was sad or hurt or angry, we knew it. If she had played a ten-year-old novice at poker, she would have lost, so I could easily detect that my slowly lengthening hair was causing her anxiety. She wanted all three of her sons to find a job where they wore a tie to work, and she thought that no bank, or 'city cooncil', or indeed any self-respecting 'proffeshinil' employer would offer a position to a boy with hair hanging over his shirt collar. I tolerated jibes like 'Look at the state o' ye – ye look like a lassie' and helpful advice along the lines of 'That Cliff Richard is real "with it". Ye should style yer hair like him' with tight-lipped stoicism.

But the final explosion came when I returned home wearing my Cuban-heeled Beatle boots for the first time. The two-inch heels forced me to walk like a flamingo that had downed a whole bottle of Johnnie Walker. I could barely negotiate a set of three steps without wobbling uncontrollably, although I honestly believed that I looked really 'fab'. After all, I was the fifth Beatle: John, George, Paul, Ringo and Willie. I tripped over the back-door step in my cool boots and Mum looked at me as if I'd just asked to borrow her best dress for the evening. At that time, mums thought that men with a haircut different from the Prussian infantry, or wearing dubious 'high heels' were a threat to the well-being of every 'decent' teenager in Britain.

'Oh, my God' was as much as she could gulp out as an opener, but she soon recovered, and off we sped on the carousel I'd ridden so many times before. 'Whit the bloody hell d'ye think ye look like? Fowk will point an' laugh at ye in the street. It's bad enough wi' that hair o' yours withoot this.' She swept the back of her hand in the general direction of my feet. 'Weel, m'lad, ye're no' goin' oot that door lookin' like the village idiot. Yer father will hae them things in the bin as soon as he sees them.'

I knew it was pointless trying to argue, but the adolescent pride cells in my teenage brain blurted out, 'Ah paid fur them masel'. Anyhow, Ah dinna tell ye whit kind o' shoes tae wear or how tae style yer hair. How aboot you leave me to dae whit Ah want an' Ah'll leave you tae dae whit you want? Eh?' Even as I was saying the words, I knew that I was out of line and it would only make things worse. My mum looked straight into me and her eyes flickered tribal Celtic anger and frustration in equal measure. I realised I'd made a big mistake and before she could erupt, I took her hands in mine. 'Ah'm sorry, Mum,' I said. 'Ah ken ye're tryin' tae protect me an' Ian an' wee Gerald fae the evils o' the wurld, but we can tak' care o' oorsel's an' each other now, an' we need tae explore oor ain lives. Ye need tae let go a wee bit now, Mum.'

She shook her head and ruffled my hair. 'Ye always were a headstrong wee boy, Billy.'

When I heard her call me by the name she'd stopped using when I started primary school, I was a hair's breadth from ripping the stupid, precious boots off my feet and throwing them in the bin myself.

It was good being 'Willie', the Beatle-boot-wearing grown-up milk laddie. But it was difficult to forget how safe it had felt to be 'Billy', the wee boy cuddling into his mum while the iodine stung his skinned knee.

We sat for a couple of minutes holding hands and saying nothing. Then Mum went up to the bathroom to compose herself. Ten seconds later, my dad came in through the back door.

'Hi, Dad,' I said, without turning round. The smell of pine and mahogany that permeated the kitchen announced him as clearly as any telegram.

He walked over to the sink and began to fill the kettle. 'Is that the kind o' boots you young lads are wearin' nowadays?' He smiled and shook his head. 'Ye look ridiculus. Get twa cups.'

*

'Whit are ye daein' the moarn's night, Wullie?' George Beattie inquired from the next urinal, taking great care to look up at the ceiling and well away from anything that might send me the wrong signals.

George was the school heart-throb, the male equivalent of Maureen Duncan, and he had a breathless following among a huge number of females in the school, not all of whom were pupils. If Kirkton High had been in Texas, George would have been the hunky quarterback and Maureen would have been Prom Queen.

'Nuthin' much, dode. How?' I responded suspiciously, gazing at a completely different patch of toilet ceiling.

'Ah've asked Mo Duncan tae come fur a wee walk wi' me up the Emmock Woods the moarn's night, but she says she'll no' go withoot her mate Muggie.'

I gave it a little shake and replaced it in my trousers with a flourish, as though I was a Samurai sheathing his sword. 'So ye want me tae come wi' ye so I can keep Muggie occupied while ye get fresh wi' Maureen?'

'Aye, Wullie, it wid mak' it a kind o' foursum', like.'

This all sounded highly dicey. Why had quarterback George picked me? Besides, what would Margaret think about me tagging along like a spare prick? I decided to go straight for it with George. 'How come ye're askin' me, dode? It's no' as if we're that close mates. Nae offence. So how are ye askin' me tae come wi' yez? As if that's no' enough, whit d'ye think Muggie'll dae if Ah wiz tae turn up saying, "Ah wiz jist passin' an' Ah've decided tae join yez on yer stroll"?'

Dode smiled. 'Ye dinna understand, Wullie. Mo telt me that Muggie kind o' fancies ye an' she widnae be averse tae you comin' alang the moarn's night.'

I was flabbergasted. In the two and a half years since I first set eyes on spotty Margaret Strachan she had transformed from a big ugly ducking into a wee swan. She had done all her vertical growing at primary school, and the same rampant hormones that had produced her spotty complexion and resulted in many tearful evenings being cuddled by her mum now provided a face and a body that were well worth the wait. She was beautiful.

But hold on just a wee minute. How would Margaret Strachan possibly fancy me when she could get just about any boy in the school dancing to her tune if she wanted? Was George setting me up? Were Margaret and Maureen going to have a great big joke at my expense when I turned up for the walk and twenty of our classmates appeared from behind trees to point at me and laugh at my gullibility? Was it really worth the risk of public humiliation? Oh, yes.

'OK, dode,' I said, trying to look cool. 'Ah'll dae ye the favour. Whit time are ye meetin' them?'

So, by default, I had a date with Margaret Strachan for seven o'clock the next evening, and by half past six

I had completed my efforts to look like the lead singer in a 1960s pop group, with my cherished Beatle boots rounding off the look. Ten minutes later, I was at the rendezvous point on the edge of the narrow road that ran into the woods, and for the next twenty minutes I just stood in the gloom, getting steadily colder and looking at my watch every ninety seconds or so, till eventually George appeared bang on seven. We barely had time to exchange pleasantries when Maureen and Margaret strolled out of the growing darkness towards their dream dates for the evening.

When we first moved to Kirkton from our grey tenement in the middle of the grey streets in the middle of the grey city, it was the green leaves and the green grass that made the biggest impact on me. There were trees all over the place: mature trees along the Kingsway and covering the railway embankment; little trees tied to stakes in the open spaces between the houses and shops, and in the playgrounds of the primary schools. When me and my little brother Ian first explored the woods north of our housing estate, we felt like we had been rehoused in Borneo. A million kinds of exotic flowers, plants, bushes, grasses and trees formed an impenetrable jungle like Tarzan lived in, and every few hundred yards we discovered another tiny light-dappled glade overflowing with bunches of wild daffodils that we could just pick for nothing and take home to our mum. It was as if the world was opening up boundless possibilities right in front of me.

Now here I was entering the same woods again, but this time with Muggie Strachan instead of my wee brother. I had the same premonition that boundless possibilities were opening up as we started to stroll along the road, with George and Maureen gradually putting a little bit of distance between them and us. Mind you, I also had a growing sense of apprehension, because after we'd come only a couple of hundred yards, I was fast running out of things to say. I didn't know what girls talked about or what they were interested in: I'd never needed to bother finding out. I tried impressing her with anecdotes from the milk lorry, but that went nowhere. I told her about the time I fell off a concrete air-raid shelter behind the tenement where we used to live, and described in detail the surgical procedures used to repair my splintered nose and cheekbones, but that went down even worse.

In desperation, I asked her if she liked 'Please Please Me', the latest Beatles' record, which had been released a couple of months earlier, and the effect was dramatic. She sparked into life and started telling me how she and Maureen had saved up between them and bought it only two weeks after it was released, and how they listened to it endlessly on the little record player in her room. This was amazing: if the two of them hadn't been lassies, they would have been just like me and Gordon. Once again the Beatles had exerted their influence over me, and I silently thanked the four of them for saving what could have been a disaster for my image and reputation.

'Did ye see them on *Thank Yer Lucky Stars*, then, Mugg— er, Margaret?'

She closed her eyes and gave a long, soft sigh. 'Wir they no' jist brilliant? Ah coudnae take ma eyes aff Paul; he looks that sensitive.'

Although I wasn't totally sure what she was talking about, I knew that my best chance lay in playing along, so I tried to look as wistful as she did and replied, 'Oh, aye. He diz look sensitive, right enough.'

That must have been the right answer because she moved close, took my arm and confided, 'Paul's eyes are that dreamy, Ah fairly melt when Ah look at them. Ah've got twenty-sivin posters o' him on ma bedroom wa', ye ken.'

As she spoke, her grip on my arm tightened and she snuggled right against me. I could feel her warm breath against my neck and her soft tits against my forearm, and suddenly there didn't seem to be a frosty nip in the air any more. George and Maureen had stopped about ten yards ahead and were obviously getting past the pleasant-conversation stage, so I started to guide Muggie off the road and into the woods. Once we were a couple of yards into the trees, I took my courage in both hands, turned her round and kissed her inexpertly on the lips.

I'd half expected to be shoved violently backwards on my arse, or at best that she would pull away looking aghast and indignant, but instead she closed her arms round me and began to kiss back with genuine passion, pressing her body against mine as if she couldn't get close enough. I couldn't believe my luck, but deep down, despite my lack of experience, I sort of knew that this wasn't the way girls usually behaved on a first date. Maybe I'd underestimated myself, though. Maybe I was much more attractive to girls than I'd realised. Maybe my kiss had inflamed—

Then it dawned on me. She wasn't kissing me at all; she was kissing Paul McCartney. She was locked in a passionate schoolgirl embrace with her idol, and was getting more and more turned on as she drifted deeper into her fantasy. This was fine by me at the start, but as we got more intimate, I started to wish that Muggie was making this journey with me alone, without the benefit of ever-so-sensitive Paul McCartney at my shoulder. But when her mouth opened against mine and I felt half my body's blood supply being rerouted from my brain to my reproductive organs, my whole mindset changed. I didn't have to do anything – good old Paul was doing it all for me – so if I couldn't get there on my own, what did it matter if I was getting some help from a Beatle? After all, Muggie was getting as much out of all this as me.

Things were getting into seriously uncharted territory for me now, and I was seeing things and doing things that I'd only heard about from conversations that some of the lads had while playing cards in the school toilets. I'd gone way past caring whether Paul McCartney was playing any part in this; all I knew was that I could well be walking out of these woods a whole lot more grown-up than when I walked in. Then I noticed the strangest look coming over Muggie's face, like somebody recovering after they'd been knocked unconscious.

'Don't, Wullie. We hae tae stop,' she said, wriggling half a step away. 'We've gone far too far already.'

It felt as if we had held hands and jumped off the diving board, only for her to decide halfway down that she didn't like the look of the water after all. I tried my best to persuade her that the water would be wonderful, honest, but she was quickly coming out of her hypnotic trance and none of my tender whisperings or pleadings had any effect. Inside, I felt like shouting, 'Ye canna dae this! Ah'm Paul Mc-fuckin'-Cartney. In fact, Ah'm onybody that ye want me tae be fur as long as ye want me tae be, only dinna stop now, fur Christ's sake – this is as close as Ah've ivir been,' but neither Paul nor Jesus could get her back. The moment was gone.

My body temperature and pulse rate slowly returned to normal as I leaned against a tree, with blood reluctantly coming back to my brain. Muggie readjusted herself, buttoned up all her clothes, cuddled against me and lit a cigarette.

How can girls be so in control? I thought. How can she be so cool after being so hot? I'll never understand what makes them work.

'Wullie?' she said softly through a haze of cigarette smoke.

'Whit?' I grunted, trying not very hard to disguise my frustration.

'Thank ye fur respectin' me. Ah ken it must hae been difficult fur ye tae stop, but it wiz difficult fur me an' a'.'

I'd never know what went on inside girls' heads, but in this I believed her. She was just like me, only different. She looked so emotional that maybe she really was telling me the truth, and maybe some blood had been redirected from her brain too.

Ach, well, I thought. At least the Beatles helped me take a tiny wee step into the world of sex, drugs and rock 'n' roll. OK, so it's only a 'very nearly got there' with Muggie Strachan against a tree, a nostril full of her second-hand Gold Leaf fag smoke and a meaningful discussion about the merits of 'Please Please Me', but it's a start.

On the way back down the road, Margaret clung on to me and warbled happily about how she was looking forward to going to Butlin's with her mum and dad and her wee sister in the summer, and did I like Helen

Shapiro's new hairstyle? I was as interested in all this as she had been in my broken nose, but it was obvious that she was trying to find ways of making a connection, just like I had been trying earlier. I found myself holding her close and making interested-sounding noises as she enlightened me about who fancied who and what Jennifer had told Morag that Elspeth had told Maureen.

As we got closer to the streetlights on the edge of the city, I caught a glimpse of her face and remembered the big, awkward, primary-school-uniformed, spotty girl who had given Gordon and me so much cause for laughter. I was glad that Muggie and me hadn't made it all the way into the water, even though I was sure it would have been wonderful, right enough. I actually felt quite nervous asking her if she wanted to go to the pictures with me on Saturday, and elated when she agreed.

'How did ye get on, then, Wullie?' asked George, as we left the girls at their doors and walked home together.

'No' much,' I said.

George smiled broadly. 'Ah could hae telt ye that. Ye'll get fuck a' fae her, no' even a feel o' her tits on the ootside. So whit did she gie ye, then?'

I was fed up of this oaf, for all he looked like Adonis. 'Fuck all,' I said. 'No' even a feel o' her tits on the ootside.'

That Saturday evening as I spotted Muggie walking from the bus-stop towards our rendezvous point beside the city square, I felt a little bit of genuine affection for her. She looked grown-up, relaxed and sexy, and I whispered a silent thank-you to quarterback George, the posing, selfish plonker who had inadvertently made this possible.

I suggested to Margaret that we should go to Green's Playhouse, which was showing a film that promised to be full of love scenes and weeping, so I thought it would be the kind of film Muggie would like, because it reminded me of the kind of stuff my mum enjoyed. Besides, Green's was by far the most opulent cinema in the city, having retained almost all of its original art deco fittings and fixtures. A walk through the vast marble and mosaic foyer alone was enough to impress any young lady.

The other deciding factor was that the Gaumont was screening an X-rated film depicting how the population of a small town in Texas were devoured by aliens who looked remarkably like earthlings with plastic alligator heads. Attractive as this film seemed, I couldn't have dealt with the humiliation if the woman in the ticket booth had said, 'You can come in, dear, but yer wee brother's too young.'

Amazingly, though, Muggie said she didn't really care what we saw and she would go wherever I wanted. I almost blurted out excitedly that a rerun of *Sands of*

Iwo Jima was on at the Capital, but realised in the nick of time that this wasn't Gordon I was with. So I contentedly sat through the weepy film, with my arm round Muggie, as I awkwardly scooped mouthfuls of Neapolitan Dairy Cup while she 'sooked' on the orange mivvie that I'd bought during the interval from a woman walking backwards down the central isle with a huge tray of frozen goodies and fags strapped to her middle.

I went out with Margaret Strachan about twice a week for the next two months, but it became clearer with each date that I was fifteen going on fourteen, and she was fifteen going on nineteen. Although we were worlds apart and had next to nothing in common, I really enjoyed being with her. She was warm and sensitive and caring, and I slowly began to discover a wee bit about the complexities of the female mind. Unfortunately, I probably reinforced her appreciation of the simplicities of the male mind, so the end came one warm Saturday evening in late spring.

Two young lovers sit on a little stone dyke beside the banks of the Dighty Burn where it flows along the edge of the Emmock Woods, near the place where they had their first tender liaison. Clear water gurgles gently through the rocks in mid-stream and laps over the pebbles on the bank at their feet, the setting sun burnishing the tree branches bright gold and copper.

If ever there was a 'Rabbie Burns moment', this was it. Only the sound of 'Ah think we should stop seein' each other, Wullie' drifting past my right ear stopped me from bursting into a couple of verses of 'Flow Gently, Sweet Afton'.

Through my misty romantic dream I heard someone who sounded just like me saying, 'Whit wiz that ye said, Muggie?' slashing the idyllic Victorian painting into shreds and dumping me back into north Kirkton reality.

'That's whit Ah mean, Wullie.' Muggie turned her head dramatically away. 'Ye never really listen tae me. Ah tell ye things an' ye jist dinna understand.'

She was getting a bit emotional now, but I couldn't say anything helpful because I didn't know what she was talking about, so I tried to let my body language speak for me and adopted a 'wounded and rejected' posture while she delivered the killer blow.

'Ah tried tae break it tae ye last night when we were at the pictures, but ye'd fell asleep. Ah hae tae say this now. It's fur the best.'

I could see she was summoning up the courage to deliver the *coup de grâce* as the howling Roman mob made 'thumbs-down' gestures from the terrace.

'Ah dinna want tae go oot wi' ye any mair, Wullie,' she whispered.

So in that short sentence, Muggie Strachan and me were an item no more. Never mind. I consoled myself with the thought that if Paul McCartney and Rabbie Burns couldn't do it between them, what chance did Willie Robertson have? As we walked out of the woods and back into the real world, I wiped away the warm tears running down her cheeks with the back of my hand. Behind us, the empty wee stone dyke and the sparkling waters of the Dighty Burn settled back to wait for the next couple.

Chapter Nine

The Army Cadets

'*Nemo me impune lacessit.*'

'Whit diz that mean, sir?'

'It means "No one assails me with impunity", lad.'

'Oh, right. But whit diz that really mean, though?'

'It means "Naebody fucks aboot wi' me an' gets awa' wi' it."'

'That's better. Sounds fine tae me, sir.'

When I was at primary school, the most popular leisure activities among the boys were football and pretending to be soldiers, which was hardly surprising since all the comics we read featured a hero who either scored the winning goal for Somewherechester Rovers or single-handedly wiped out a Japanese machine-gun nest and saved his whole platoon. So our playground football games were always between two sides – Scotland and the 'Inglish' – and our soldier games invariably involved us splitting into two groups, taking on the roles of 'Britishers' and 'Jerries', running about with wooden rifles or plastic machine guns, and making realistic rifle- and machine-gun-firing noises. We tried to vary the format by sometimes being US marines, or Japs, or commandoes, or paratroopers, but no matter which theatre of war we were operating in, every game had the same predictable format: everybody had unlimited 'armunishun', nobody admitted to being hit unless the muzzle was about three inches from their head, and the Britishers always slaughtered everybody else.

However, this sort of childish behaviour just wasn't acceptable once we started secondary school. Running around with toy guns was kids' stuff and not nearly exciting or dangerous enough for lads who were beginning to feel the full effects of their very own testosterone-production plant. We tried assaulting each other with various fireworks around 'Guy Fox' time as a way of adding realism to our war games, but it was becoming clear to us all that playing soldiers in the street was no fun any more. No amount of penny-banger hand grenades thrown at the Japs, or firework-rocket bazookas shot from odd bits of iron pipe at the Waffen SS could bring back the adrenaline rush of our wooden rifles and plastic machine guns. We needed another focus for our martial inclinations.

Ian McClelland was a hard little bastard and a gym teacher at Kirkton High School. He was only about five foot eight, but he just had to look at you once and you knew who was in charge and why the Germans called Scottish soldiers 'poisoned dwarfs'. He'd been a paratrooper in the Second World War and ran his PE classes like they did in 1942, when rows of young men in baggy black shorts and tight white vests jumped up and down in unison, throwing their arms out to the side. His lesson plans always followed pretty much the same pattern: 'Class 2A4, there is a beanbag on the floor in front o' each of ye. Ah will tell ye when tae pick it up an' then Ah will tell ye whit Ah want ye tae do next. STAND STILL, THAT BOY! What don't ye understand, laddie? Is waiting till ye're told tae pick up the beanbag confusing ye, or don't ye understand the words "then I'll tell ye what to do"?'

Nevertheless, Ian was really a closet saint; he was hard as nails on the outside but had a centre like a Creme Egg. He genuinely cared about the physical and mental welfare of the kids he was responsible for, and may well have earned an OBE for his contribution to keeping young boys out of Borstal if he had worked in a school in Essex. But he didn't; he taught at Kirkton High in Dundee at a time when it wasn't very sexy to work in a school that had the usual problems of an early 1960s comprehensive in the middle of a sprawling housing estate, and where there were always fights in the playground, toilets and classrooms, and where teachers got abused and assaulted by pupils and parents on a regular basis.

Despite the hostile conditions in which Ian McClelland worked, never once was there any problem in his department. We all knew that if we were daft enough to go head to head, he would break our jaw and swear we fell off the wall bars. When our dad came in to remonstrate, Ian would break his jaw as well and swear he slipped on the wet floor of the changing room. We also knew he would have got away with it too, because his defence would be unassailable. 'Your Honour, my client fought for his country in the Parachute Regiment during the Second World War and was decorated for his actions during the ill-fated attack on Arnhem Bridge. He has been a teacher of physical education for the last sixteen years and now teaches at Kirkton High School, where he devotes much of his spare time to organising after-school sports activities for his pupils and even finds time to run a detachment of the local Army Cadet Force. In addition, forty-seven of his former pupils will testify that my client's guidance, advice and support rescued each of them from a life of crime, and helped them to become qualified PE instructors or junior officers in our nation's armed forces.

'Compare this, if you will, Your Honour with my client's accuser: a fat scumbag who has never done an honest day's work in his whole life and buys his excessive weekly intake of fags and beer using the taxes paid by decent, hard-working citizens such as my client, and of course your good self, m'lud.' No contest.

Of course, Ian would never have harmed a kid in a million years, or assaulted anybody, but perception is always more powerful than reality, so he never had to.

Every Tuesday at about a quarter to four, a metamorphosis took place in the staff changing rooms at Kirkton High School, and Mr McClelland, PE instructor, became Captain McClelland, officer in the Army Cadet Force. We knew he had to leave school just after four o'clock so he could walk to the reservists' barracks up the road and get everything ready in time for the cadets, though none of us was sure what they actually did during these Tuesday-night sessions. What we did know was that when you joined the cadets, you got a proper soldier's uniform and were allowed to get your hands on real guns. This had to be the ultimate substitute for wooden rifles and plastic machine guns, so one day me and Gordon asked Mr McClelland how old you had to be to join. 'Aboot yer age,' he said, and that was that: we became boy soldiers.

Pathé newsreels at the cinema were filled with images of our brave kilted boys exacting dreadful retribution on any upstart tin-pot warlord who dared to defy us or our friends. No wonder we thought wars were wonderful and couldn't wait to get into a second-hand uniform. Even Elvis was in the US Army, and smiled at us from under his tailored 'standard-issue' GI cap. If, however, you were compiling a programme to dissuade young lads from ever joining the British Army, you couldn't come up with anything more effective than the Army Cadet Force in 1962.

After two Tuesday-evening sessions of military training at the reservists' barracks, where we were shown advanced soldiery things like how to lace up boots and clean brass buckles, Gordon and me were handed a note from Captain McClelland and told to report to the Black Watch Barracks in the centre of the town to be issued with our uniforms. Although I'd walked past the outside of the place thousands of times, I'd never actually been behind the big stone wall that shielded military secrets from the prying eyes of wee Dundee housewives on their way home with their man's tea and unscrupulous Soviet agents on their way home with the latest intelligence reports on Dundee United's Saturday line-up.

We showed our note to the kilted soldier guarding the entrance and were ushered through the gate into the middle of the eighteenth century: the place looked like it should have been full of redcoats, and everything was made out of dark grey. The vast empty parade ground, the wall along the street, the three-storey buildings on the other two sides of the square, were all made out of hard, unrelenting grey stone.

Only the fourth side of the square offered an alternative view; beyond yet another grey stone wall, which ran down the whole length of the eastern side of the barracks, we could see a little medieval graveyard full of weeping willows and broken gravestones covered in moss. Somehow, this vista looked even more cold and pitiless than the flinty stone of the barrack buildings and the boundary walls. All the wee crosses and cherubs and angels adorning the graves filled me with a deep foreboding, as if they were saying, 'Go on, son, enlist over there and you'll soon be joining us over here.' I was certain that Gordon felt the same trepidation as me, but neither of us could ever admit to having such poofy, girlie thoughts, so the two of us put on our hard-as-nails masks and sauntered across the parade ground, trying to look as if we didn't give a shit, and headed towards a solitary light bulb illuminating that cold, empty world of grey.

After we had been passed through the light-bulb door by another sentry, this time in fatigue overalls, the two of us were ushered into a zone called the quartermaster's store. The place was a miniature aircraft hangar, complete with a massive old wooden counter and rows of seats that separated those who wanted things from those who could supply them. It smelled like the home team's changing room in the Coliseum and was bathed in fluorescent light, so we could see racks and racks of fantastic Christmas presents for pretend soldiers and disturbing-looking implements for serious soldiers.

There were four or five blokes moving among the racks of materials, all of them dressed in the same kind of drab, greasy overalls as the guy on the door. Every one of them seemed either to be sitting on a stack of materials or aimlessly wandering about with a clipboard and a huge mug of tea. Me and Gordon stood behind the big wooden counter playing at being invisible. At last one of the tea-soaked storeroom soldiers sauntered over to the desk and planted his mug on top of a pile of official-looking papers. He was obviously unconcerned that potentially top-secret documents may slowly be turning to illegible pulp below his dripping mug.

'OK, lads. Ye'll be here tae pick up yer kit, right?'

'Right, mate,' says Gordon.

The guy's eyes hardened. 'Ah'm no' yer fuckin' mate, son. Whit d'ye think these are?' He pointed towards two stripes on the sleeve of his shirt.

'That means ye're a corpurull, aye?' Gordon ventured.

'Clever lad – ye'll do well. So whit do we call men like me wi' twa stripes, then, smart lad?'

I was just about to tell him that we called men like

him with two stripes 'bullying, ignorant arseholes', but Gordon stayed calmer than me and got in first with, 'Ye get ca'd "corporal", Corporal.'

The guy was well pleased. 'Oh, ye're goin' tae dae so well, son.'

I smiled demurely at the man with two little stripes and one big attitude.

We were both allocated a complete set of military clothing and equipment, all of which had probably been rescued from Dunkirk. First, we were given a pair of trousers, which were heavy and a size too big; next, it was a shirt knitted out of steel wool, followed by a frayed khaki tie. The humiliation continued with the issue of a battledress tunic that was straight out of one of those propaganda films that cheered everybody up during the Second World War. I could almost hear George Formby squeaking out a wee song about England being impregnable because he had his little ukulele in his hand and we were going to 'give Jerry a bloody nose, eey, aye, Moother'. Next, it was a belt and gaiters, which we were instructed to regularly cover in stuff called Blanco, whatever that was, and to regularly polish the buckles and things with stuff called Brasso, whatever that was.

The final ignominy, though, was my bonnet. The Black Watch wear a dark blue bonnet with a distinctive red hackle at the side and a small red wool pom-pom, called a toorie, on the top. When the regimental cap badge is added, the effect is dramatic. One glimpse of this headgear, we were assured by our captains and a generation of Scottish music-hall singers, causes panic among our enemies and compels them to surrender in droves, just so they won't have to face screaming kilted savages who eat sheep's stomachs filled with blood and gore, and play wailing instruments fashioned from other bits of animal innards.

Unfortunately, my bonnet looked like I had a scone balanced on top of my head. It was obviously made for a six-year-old pigmy, and even Corporal Two Stripes conceded that it was 'a bit nippet'. I couldn't understand why he just couldn't go and get me another one; surely there must be more bonnets among all the racks of stuff. However, our corporal was much more pragmatic: his solution was to put the bonnet over the handle of the door and pull down to stretch the fabric. I think if he'd had a vice handy, he might have tried to reduce the size of my head in the same way. Finally, when he was happy that he'd stretched my bonnet by a millionth of an inch, he gave us each a monstrous length of something resembling brown greaseproof paper and told us to wrap up our kit to keep it dry on the way home. Then he asked us to sign something, wished us *bon voyage*, and went back to his tea.

'Whit happens if there's a waar an' it's rainin'?' Gordon asked me, as we walked back across the damp grey square hugging big, brown greaseproof bundles to our chests.

'Ah dinna ken, Goardin,' I said. 'Maybe the Russians winna want tae get their kit damp either, so naebody'll turn up fur the waar till it's a nice day.'

Things started to get a bit silly then, with Gordon playing the part of a Soviet general and me a new Black Watch cadet with a diminutive bonnet.

Gordon put his brown-paper package under one arm and started to swagger across the parade ground. 'Vat do you think, then, Enemy Comrade Villie? Should ve go for smashing all ze imperialist capitalists todayinski or should ve vait till ze glorious Soviet sun rises over ze Balkans?'

'Nuthin' beats a bit o' Soviet sunshine on yer Balkans, Goardinski,' I replied. 'Ah think we should gie it a miss till tomorrow so that our Balkans can warm up a bit.'

'Very vell, little Englishinski soldier from Scotlandski. I vill hold back my massed divisions till ze sky is a vee bit brighterski.'

'That suits me fine, Comrade General Ivan Goardinski,' I said. 'But answer me ane question: whit the fuck's Blanco?'

Gordon was completely in character now and I was becoming worried that he would have me sent to Siberia. 'I do not care about zis western Blancoscavich product. My mind is at a higher level. Ven ve get out of zis place, I will form a committee of vorkers, soldiers and peasants to take over ze government.'

I wasn't convinced. 'Whit aboot the bus conductors? How come they're no' on yer committee, Comrade General Goardinski? Should it no' be a committee o' workers, skivers, trapeze artists and Blanco-rubbers tae properly reflect oor society, Brother Fellow Milk Laddie Comrade General?'

He stopped in the middle of the parade ground, turned about, and stared at me with a manic expression on his face, his hands working at the greaseproof package at his chest. For half a second, I wasn't sure whether my best friend was a gifted actor or a potential recruit for the KGB. 'Avay an' piss up a poleski, Comrade Traitor, an' stick yer trapeze artists up yer arseski.'

At least I had the comfort of knowing that Gordon's face wouldn't be on the cover of the next issue of *KGB Monthly*, and by the time we got to the exit gate I was in hysterics. Gordon was completely immersed in being a Soviet general and was adding '-ski' or '-ich' to the end of every second word, while I was giggling uncontrollably. The sentry didn't even acknowledge us, but I could tell what he was thinking from his pained expression, which said, 'God help us. It's a sad day for the British Army when we have to let little giggling schoolgirls into the ranks of the Black Watch, even if they are only kiddy-on boy soldiers.'

British Army boots, however, were definitely not to be giggled about. They have long been renowned for being among the worst items of military equipment ever devised, and were designed for the sole purpose of showing how well our armed forces could polish things. When it came to impressing the Queen Mother on a march past, or showing the barefoot heathen hordes how a real army polishes its toecaps, then our boots were just the thing. Her Majesty could wave serenely at the results of hundreds of mouthfuls of glistening spit mixed with black polish, while several medal-encrusted presidents from obscure countries stood on the podium beside her and trembled at the sight of so much shininess in the ranks.

Although it was designed to perfection for kicking colonial miscreants up the arse, in every other department the British Army boot was totally useless. It was unforgiving in its toe-crushing hardness, it hurt your feet and gave you blisters, it was too heavy, too short, and it soaked up water like a sponge. Worst of all, the steel heel- and toecaps and the dozens of steel hobnails in the soles meant that you slid all over the place like a baby penguin on pack ice whenever your feet encountered a hard surface. Thanks to my grannie Brannan, my mother's mother, I sported a fine pair of Second World War army boots almost as soon as I was issued with my uniform and undersized bonnet.

At five foot one, my 'big' grannie Brannan towered over my 'wee' grannie Robertson by at least ten inches; mind you, thanks to the ravages of rickets, so did everybody else in the city over the age of nine. Big Grannie Brannan overflowed with love for her children and grandchildren, but she represented the last of a generation who were conditioned to think that even the slightest flicker of emotion was weak and un-British, so Big Grannie Brannan and most of the women she knew stoically hid behind drab clothes and dour expressions, while their equally stoic men died in their hundreds of thousands advancing on German trenches. Unlike Grannie Robertson, Grannie Brannan would never have offered me a cigarette in a million years, and even scowled at my dad when he lit up.

Grannie Brannan's attitude to life was that the only people of any value in this world were the massed ranks of the working class. Everybody who was working class was her respected equal and a potential friend, regardless of race, religion, age, gender or background. However, anybody who didn't fall within this socio-economic band was a worthless parasite living on the sweat of honest men and women. They contributed nothing, took everything, and subjugated the workers to a world of ignorance and squalor in order to feed the furnace of their own limitless greed. Mind you, it was an understandable point of view when you lived in a city at the turn of the twentieth century that lay claim to both the largest number of millionaires in the world and the most horrific poverty, slums and social deprivation anywhere in Europe.

Of all the young men from Dundee who tried to enlist in the British Army in 1904, more than half were deemed unfit for military duty, having failed the rudimentary medical test because of bronchial disease, childhood deformity, polio, malnourishment or any one of a litany of hereditary or acquired medical conditions, while the jute-baron aristocracy competed to outspend each other on good works by donating acres of parkland, marble-floored libraries, massive civic buildings and ornately tiled public lavvies for the health and enlightenment of the population they so ruthlessly exploited. So maybe Grannie Brannan had a point.

Unlike my wee grannie, who once told me that her voting tactic was that she 'gae them a' their wee cross 'cos ane's as bad as the ithir', my big grannie was a fervent socialist and very well read on the subject of politics. She would happily and eloquently articulate her views to anybody who asked. Her brother Eddie wasn't nearly as good with words, but he made his own contribution to the liberation of the oppressed masses by going off to fight in the Spanish Civil War against Franco's fascists when he was little more than a boy. I've still got his medals.

Because of my big grannie Brannan, I could recite every word of Robert Burns's 'A Man's a Man' and sing 'The Red Flag' from beginning to end by the time I was six. Thanks to my wee grannie, I could also sing 'The Old Rugged Cross' and 'Climb, Climb Up Sunshine Mountain' at the same age without missing a beat.

My mother and I were sitting on a tram one day when I was about seven. I was singing away to myself with my nose against the window as we clanked and electrically sparked the short distance from the city centre to the tenement where we lived. An old man sitting behind us gently tapped my mum on the shoulder, apologised for the intrusion, and said, 'It restores my faith when I hear a young, modern mother has taught her son the very same hymns that I was taught by my own mother when I was a boy. I've never heard such a beautifully innocent rendition of "Shall We Gather at the River".'

My mum smiled demurely and graciously accepted the compliment, although she couldn't have recited a single line. It had been my wee grannie's turn to look after us the evening before, so Ian and I had been practising the Salvation Army songs that moved her so much, including 'Shall We Gather at the River'. I even smacked my wee soft palms against the wooden seat of the tramcar in time to the beat when it came to the chorus: 'Yes, we will gather at the river . . .'

If it had been my big grannie's turn to babysit the previous night, I would have been inciting the whole bus to revolution with my full-blooded, seven-year-old rendition of 'Arise, Ye Workers, From Your Slumbers' with my nose against the window, and fervently trying to convince the old man that religion was the 'opiate of the people' and 'nothing but a ploy of the ruling classes to subjugate and enslave the producers of all wealth'.

My wee grannie would try to teach me about her saviour Jesus, and my big grannie would try to teach me about her saviour Karl Marx. It certainly helps to have a balanced childhood, but life isn't a monochrome production. Yin and yang look dead artistic on rice paper, whirling round each other in their stark black and white, but where's the huge multicoloured mush in the middle that represents how the world really works? Where's the muddled-up truth?

Wee Grannie and her host of siblings weren't entirely apprentice angels, despite daily climbing up sunshine mountain with 'faces all a-glow'. Not because of any shred of malice in them, but through sheer 'ignorance' in the literal and kindest definition of the word. When she looked after us to let my mum and dad go to the pictures, she told us stories at bedtime that left us lying rigid in the dark with our eyes wide open, terrified to go to sleep. 'As the bairn lay sleepin',' she would purr, 'an auld wizzined wummin wi' nae head come doon through a hole in the ceilin' whisperin' the words "Follay me, follay me, follay me me meeeeeeeeee." ' It didn't occur to me to question how she could have whispered anything if she had no head, because the terror was too overwhelming. Just the thing for a six-year-old and a four-year-old at bedtime.

Her many brothers and sisters were every bit as caringly insensitive. On the night before Christmas Eve, we were being looked after by Wee Grannie so that mum and dad could go out to a local Christmas dance with a couple of their friends. Our uncle Stuart was coming up to our two-room tenement flat for his supper, and Ian and me were really looking forward to seeing him because he always made us laugh. He worked in a sawmill, and three and a bit fingers of his left hand were missing by degrees. The circular saw had amputated his little finger completely, sliced through his ring finger below the first knuckle, then continued its whistling, blood-spurting track to remove the top half of his middle finger and the tip of his index finger.

Despite this impediment, he was a real hit on the piano accordion, and kept us kids awake until well past our bedtime at birthdays, weddings, New Year, Christmas, christenings and every other family occasion with a mixture of loud Scottish ceilidh music that bounced around the walls of the wee tenement living room, and a liberal supply of morbid fascination at how his mutilated left-hand stumps danced over the keys.

When he arrived, we always jumped on him, while he made a great fuss of our little brother, Gerald, who crawled to him over the warm linoleum. Between sips of tea, Stuart casually mentioned to Wee Grannie that he was sorry to be a bit late getting here, but he'd been witness to a dreadful accident down the road at the West Port. Ian and me were playing with Gerald, who was gurgling away in front of the fire, and weren't really listening, until Uncle Stuart started to describe the incident in detail. It seemed that a tramcar had collided with a reindeer-drawn sleigh and that bits of sledge, dead reindeer and mangled Christmas presents were strewn all over the bottom of the Blackness Road.

Ian and me stared at each other in growing disbelief as Uncle Stuart went on. 'Och, it wiz carnidge, Dolly.' He spoke to Wee Grannie as if we weren't there. 'There wiz an auld man wi' a white beard an' red claithes crushed under the runners o' the sledge an' the wheels o' the tram, an' a bonny wee reindeer wi' its neck broke wiz lyin' ower his legs. Ye could see its wee red nose pokin' oot under the sledge. Whit a shame. Och, weel, nivir mind. Is there ony mair tea in the pot?' Ian and me went into hysterics. It took Wee Grannie half the night to convince us that her brother had invented the whole 'amusing' tale.

Big Grannie's vision of a socialist utopia wasn't the inspiration for John Lennon's 'Imagine', but she did teach her grandchildren to respect the dignity of every human being, and to defy those who had sent three of our wee grannie's brothers to their senseless deaths at the Somme. She also encouraged us to fight against a system that gave stupid men power only because of rank or privilege. Or, in the words of her beloved Rabbie Burns, 'Sense an' worth o'er a' the earth shall bear the gree an' a' that.' I didn't realise at the time, but this is the philosophy that made the Scots, under the shadow of the Union Flag of course, able to colonise half the world. But only after finishing their milk round.

Wee Grannie Robertson was unconditional with her emotions, whereas big Grannie Brannan held hers in an iron grip. So, like all children, my brothers and I gravitated towards where there were no rules, no restrictions and unrestricted laughter. My big grannie expressed her love through watching the joy on our faces when she could give us something she knew we really needed, material or otherwise. Like most working-class widows living on her own at that time, she didn't have a whole lot of money coming in, but she was thrifty and always seemed able to put something aside so she could present us with a surprise. One day, out of the blue, she handed me a pair of second-hand army-surplus boots as a present for joining the Army Cadet Force and doing my bit for my country. She must have asked my mum for the size of my feet because they fitted perfectly.

At the beginning of November, Captain McClelland, disguised as plain Mr McClelland, PE teacher, told us that we had to wear our cadet uniforms to school on Armistice Day, and we were to parade in the playground outside the gym hall at 0830 hours. There were about eighteen lads at the school who were in the cadets by that time, so McClelland must have thought it would be appropriate if they made an effort to mark the day. Gordon and me thought it was a nice touch and would give us a chance to swagger about a bit. The problem was that it's easy to get carried away when you're an adolescent boy looking forward to a good swagger, so we managed to convince each other that we should wear our uniforms for the whole day. It would show our commitment to Armistice Day, and save us the bother of changing once we'd finished the milk round. After all, it would be tight to get home after the round, get changed and get to the school by eight thirty. This way, we could go straight from the depot to the playground parade.

So the next morning, Gordon, who had by now bought his own boots, and me crunched through the pitch darkness in correct military fashion on our way to the depot, feeling mighty pleased with ourselves and pretty damned cocky in our full uniform and polished tackety boots.

Johnny was just finishing his breakfast fag near the gate, so he was the first person to see us and he nearly set fire to himself. 'Fur fuck's sake,' was all he could think of, followed rapidly by, 'Quick, lads, c'mere tae ye see this twa,' shouted back in the general direction of the truck.

Steevie and Si were the first to arrive, pursued by Avril, who wanted to see what the commotion was about. Even Sabre sensed that something wasn't right, and sat menacingly motionless, growling very softly in the back of his throat.

'If Ah'd kent it wiz fancy dress, Ah wid've come as a Viking,' said Steevie.

'If it wiz fancy dress, ye could've come as yersel',' quipped Si. 'A'body wid ken instantly ye'd come as a wee Dundee chancer.'

'Fuck off,' Steevie wittily retorted.

Avril seemed at a loss for words. 'Whit the bloody hell's a' this?' she said, waving the back of her hand over the sight in front of her.

'We're markin' Armistis Day,' I said proudly. 'We wur telt tae wear oor uniforms.'

Avril looked incredulous. 'On a mulk roond?' she said. 'Whit stupit bastard wid tell laddies tae dae a daft thing like that?'

'Well, he didnae akchully say tae wear it on oor roond, Avril,' Gordon began to try to give some sort of explanation. 'Y'see, we've tae be on parade at—' Gordon stopped abruptly as Steevie, Si and Johnny had gone beyond smiling and entered the wonderful land of hysterical laughter.

Avril was shaking her head and Sabre was glaring straight at us, clearly unimpressed by our khaki uniforms, and unconcerned that we might be seasoned commandoes with years of unarmed combat training behind us. Fat Boab and Wee Good hadn't arrived at the depot yet – their pleasure at our discomfort was still to come – but the rest didn't need to wait for additional support.

'Right, men!' Johnny proclaimed in his best sergeant-major voice. 'Private Devlin, you camulfladge the larry wi' green pent. An' you, Private Malcolm, cut a big roond hole in the raif o' Auld Jim's cab so wi' can set up oor masheen gun.'

Gordon and me just stood there feeling more and more foolish as the lads laughed. This wasn't going according to the script at all. Even Avril was smiling now and Sabre had visibly relaxed.

Fat Boab and Wee Good John then arrived together. It was still only ten to five, so they just sort of sauntered into the depot without a care in the world, until Boab saw me and Gordon in the light of the lamp on the shed. His jaw dropped, almost spilling semi-eaten

211

crisps down his chin. Fat Boab was the only person in the world who devoured crisps without even realising what flavour they were, and ate little sugary sweets called Love Hearts without first reading the tiny loving message on each. The only one that would have moved him if he'd bothered to read it was the sweet that had the words 'I'm yours' printed on it. That would appeal to Boab, who would definitely think, Richt ye are, before shoving it into his mouth with six others.

Anyway, Boab was clearly worried. Rules, regulations and protocol were the very foundation of his whole belief system, and he looked pleadingly at Gordon, then me, then Wee Good, then Sabre, then Avril, then back to Gordon and me again, until he eventually managed to say, 'Should Ah hae on ma Boys' Brigade uniform? Is this iffishul fae the cooncil or the kirk or somethin'?'

'Dinna worry, Boab,' said Johnny through his laughter. 'It's jist them twa balloons celibratin' Armistrust Day. If it hud been iffishul, yer dad wid hae telt ye, and Wee Good wid hae hud on his Girl Guide uniform.'

Everybody except Wee John chuckled, even the two boy soldiers, but I registered Johnny's fleeting glance at the wee man and wondered what perverse images were flashing through his head.

If our arrival at the depot quickly showed us that we'd made an embarrassing mistake, the round itself was an unmitigated disaster. Gordon and me slipped and slithered all over the place, trying to keep upright holding our carriers. Getting on and off the lorry was the worst part, since there was almost no traction on the road at all when we stepped backwards off the moving truck, and when we tried to get back on, our boots skidded hopelessly on the steel surface of the step. It's a miracle one of us wasn't killed.

Gordon and me were slowing the deliveries down something dreadful. We couldn't run fast, get on and off fast, and were a positive danger to the rest of the crew, so it was little wonder that the lads were getting pissed off. Gordon and me were also getting angry with ourselves for being so stupid. Tension mounted with every delivery. Today, it was always either Gordon or me who was the last back at the lorry, and Jim even had to stop several times to wait for one or both of us. This was unprecedented, and I could see the frustration in Gordon as, like me, he tried hard to keep up to his normal speed.

After one particularly long run through the pre-fabs in Blackshade, I arrived at the rendezvous point to find the lorry, with its full complement, stopped and waiting for me. Normally, I would have been there with at least a minute and a half to spare before the lorry cruised past and I leaped lightly on to the step, so I forced myself into a sprint, which I hoped would minimise the delay and my own humiliation. Bad move.

By the time I reached the step, I was already marginally out of control, and the final ill-timed jump robbed me of the little that remained. I thumped into the back of the lorry too fast and too high, so that I hit the back step at an awkward angle. My right boot skidded off the steel surface, flew upwards, and hit Steevie just below his knee. He howled in shocked pain and slid off the step on to the road, curling into a ball and clutching his leg.

Despite years of conditioning as a streetwise survivor, tears leaked from the sides of his screwed-up eyes and I thought he was going to pass out, but after a few seconds he pulled himself to his knees, glared up at me and shouted, 'Ye stupit bastard. Ye could hae broke ma fuckin' leg, ye daft bastard. You an' yer stupit clumpy baits.' He held on tightly to his knee and slowly pulled himself to his feet, grimacing at the pain. 'Ah should rip them aff ye afore ye cripple somebody.'

My own frustration and testosterone took over and I reacted the way all young men have reacted ever before and ever since: raw aggression. 'Come on, then, Steevie,' I said. 'Come an' rip them aff me.'

I saw the same cold, focused look come into his eyes that I'd seen in Sabre's only three hours before, and knew that this was probably going to be my second big mistake of the day.

'YOU TWA.' The tone demanded instant obedience. Steevie, me, every other laddie on the truck and a couple of kids in bed in a nearby pre-fab instantly froze. Avril pointed at the two of us, and the sheer authority in her voice explained why a powerful canine killing machine would stand stock still at her side, waiting for the snap of her fingers, while his every instinct was sending his quivering body straight towards the enemy's throat. 'Git back on this larry NOW!'

Once everybody was back on the step and Auld Jim had floored the accelerator, Avril continued, 'Every ane o' yez'll work thigither tae git this roond feenished in the next half 'oor, richt? First, git the roond feenished an' then yez can kick the shit oot o' each ithir in yer ain time.'

The rest of the round was completed in virtual silence, with Steevie and me barely acknowledging each other, even when the rotation required us to be standing together at the huddin' rail. When we eventually got back to the depot, about fifteen minutes behind schedule, and stood down off the step, I could see that the rest of the lads were glancing apprehensively at each other, obviously wondering if anything would start between Steevie and me.

I looked my potential adversary straight between the eyes. 'Ah'm sorry Ah clattered yer leg an' ye got hurt. Ah honestly didnae mean it. But if ye still want a square go, that's fine wi' me.'

There was no way that I would last more than thirty

seconds in a 'square go' with Steevie Devlin. I'd seen him in action in the playground and in the street, and he was cold, methodical and frighteningly efficient. He didn't fight people, he destroyed them, and I put it down to years of clandestine training by his dad and his big brothers. Steevie shook his head and I could see a tiny wee smile at the corners of his mouth.

'Ye're a daft bastard, Wullie, wearing stupit big tackety baits tae deliver mulk.' He was smiling broadly as we both shook hands.

Everybody visibly relaxed and Avril smiled a wee secret smile to herself.

Steevie and I lagged behind the others when we walked through the depot gates. 'That's as sair as Ah can ivir remember bein' kicked, Wullie,' said Steevie quietly. 'Ah wiz near gettin' tore richt intae ye, honest.'

'Ah ken that, Steevie, but Ah wid hae totally gone fur ye as well, though,' I said truthfully.

'Ah ken ye wid hae, Wullie,' he replied, taking a small nipper from his tobacco tin. 'But ye wid hae lost.'

Chapter Ten

The Annual Camp

Finest training in the world.

Gordon and me had managed to negotiate a whole unpaid week off to go to the annual spring army-cadet camp in Elgin. We formed three ranks along the main platform in Dundee's Central Railway Station as if we were real soldiers, and then we filed into the carriages with about a hundred other boys dressed in old Second World War uniforms to start our journey north – just like being on a proper troop train. In a great cloud of screaming whistles, black smoke and white steam, the train puffed slowly away from the platform, and the troops sat back to read *The Beano* and eat the meat-paste sandwiches that their mums had prepared.

I'd only been as far north as Arbroath before, so it came as a bit of a surprise when more and more countryside and coastline kept drifting past the carriage window. I didn't know that Scotland was so big, and began to wonder just exactly how far away Elgin was. After what seemed like for ever, the train slowed down as it clattered across a rusty bridge spanning a wide, clear river and, with a loud hissing sigh, eventually coughed into the bowels of a cavernous Victorian railway station. It was obvious from the acres of paved platforms and soaring wrought-iron arches that this place was in the centre of a pretty significant town.

'This'll be Elgin, then?' I said to Gordon in the next seat.

'Ah bloody hope so, Wullie. Ma arse is a' pins an' needles wi' a' this sittin'.'

Our hopes were dashed when somebody shouted, 'Hey, look, lads, we're in Aiburdeen.'

I was seriously disappointed that we were only about halfway to our camp and I had to face about another two hours sitting on this seat. I think that everybody in the carriage felt the same as me, because suddenly a bored voice said, 'Oh, fuck this, lads, let's git the drink oot now. Ah canna wait till we git there,' and about two dozen of the older lads began to pull open their haversacks.

They had all obviously been in the cadets for years;

some of them even wore stripes on their tunics. Clearly this wasn't their first visit to an annual camp, because they began to magic large numbers of McEwan's Export cans and half-bottles of Bell's from their rucksacks with practised aplomb, and started pouring generous mixtures of beer and whisky into metal mess cans for each other. Before the train had left 'Aiburdeen' the whole carriage was enjoying the alcoholic bounty, and Gordon and me were happily sipping the beer-and-whisky mixture with the rest. The problem was that we had no resistance at all to the demon drink and within ten minutes I was feeling light-headed, so when somebody down at the front opened the window and began to serenade the waiting commuters with an out-of-tune version of 'The Northern Lights of Old Aberdeen', Gordon and me took up the chorus with gusto. We slept through most of the rest of the journey to Elgin.

Day One, 1800 Hours: Welcome Campers

Five of the most un-military vehicles I'd ever seen greeted the train in a dilapidated row in Elgin Railway Station car park. These battered 1930s buses must have been hired by the Ministry of Defence from the town's cheapest transport company, whose only other contracts were probably ferrying migrant tattie-pickers to the outlying farms during harvest-time, and keeping hens on the seats during the winter. Thanks to the rust that held these deathtraps together, we all arrived safely at the camp. I was surprised that there wasn't a film crew from the BBC on hand to record our triumphant arrival: they could have used it to dissuade any unfriendly nation from ever thinking about taking military action against the UK. The Soviets may have flexed their muscles by parading hundreds of intercontinental ballistic missiles and tens of thousands of troops across Red Square, but we weren't to be outdone. We could show newsreel films of several dozen army cadets spilling out of rusty buses in Elgin town square. That would make Ivan think twice.

Groups of young boys are usually fairly immune to noxious odours in confined spaces, but after the half-hour ride from the railway station to the camp, we couldn't get away from the smell of farts, stale beer breath, hen shit and unwashed farm labourers quickly enough, so we were all thankful to spill out into fresh air and line up on a parade ground as big as Wales.

'How come this square's so big, Wullie? Ye could get the whole British Army standin' here,' said Gordon, gazing around at the endless prairie of concrete.

'Ye could get a'body else's armies here an' a',' I said, 'so mibbie it's in case Earth gets invaidid fae Mars an' a' the wurld's armies hae tae combine tae defend oor planitt.'

'Shut the fuck up, ye prune,' was Gordon's considered response to my suggestion. 'Ye're spendin' too much time at the Odeon.'

I could tell that we were in an established army camp, but I didn't really know what the conditions were going to be like. My last experience of camping had been about three years before, with six boys and Brian McLaren's dog in a four-man tent we had rented from Brian's big brother so we could spend a couple of days and nights exploring the Sidlaw Hills. Although I had a tent of my own, it was in the shape of a tepee and had cowboys and Indians on the fabric, so I had denied owning anything of any value to our mission, and we gave Brian's big brother sixpence each to hire his tent for a weekend. We had a wet, cold, miserable time, and Wee Good John twisted his ankle in a rabbit hole.

Back on the vast concrete square, the early-evening tranquillity was abruptly shattered. 'PARAAADE! PAAARAAAAADE, 'SHUN!' So we all shunned.

Ten minutes later, every boy had been marched off with his group to collect a thin white cotton sleeping bag and four thick woolly blankets, before being lined up again in front of what was to be his billet for the week. Captain McClelland stood in front of our squad and explained the rules, like where the toilets and showers were, where the mess was and what we were allowed and weren't allowed to do. 'Lights out at ten o'clock, lads, an' reveille – that's when ye hae tae get up – is at six.'

I could feel the sudden intake of breath from the others and could just about detect gasps of 'Six o'-fuckin'-clock in the moarnin'? That's the middle o' the bloody night, fur fuck's sake.' Gordon and me smirked at each other: for a milk laddie, this was a lie-in.

Gordon and me thought that half past nine was a late night, so by ten o'clock a combination of the unfamiliar alcohol, the excitement and the weariness of the long journey had sent both of us into a sound sleep on our little iron bunks. At half past four that next morning, the two of us were long programmed to be wide awake, and by five we had brushed our teeth, had a shit, and were getting dressed after having the hot showers to ourselves for a full fifteen minutes.

Day Two, 1400 Hours: Map-Reading

'My name is Captain Pope. That's P-O-P-E, and I've already heard every joke and song there is about me getting fucked or falling off my horse, so let's just give all that a miss, shall we? Any questions . . . ? Good. Right, for the next two hours I'll be teaching you how to read a map and use a compass. Map-reading is an essential skill for the modern soldier and a vital component in the art of survival in a hostile environment.'

This'll be useful, I thought. Beechwood's about as hostile an environment as you can get, so if I've got my map and compass with me the next time I'm collecting milk money, I should have a much higher chance of survival. Captain 'No Fucking Him, Please' Pope had set up a huge blackboard at the front of the room and had already drawn a chalk circle covering the whole board, so we could all clearly witness the mysteries he was about to reveal.

'OK,' says the map-reading guru, producing an army-issue compass, which he held out in front of him before placing it on a little table beside the blackboard. 'Can anybody tell me what this instrument is called?' Silence. 'For Christ's sake, you can't all be this thick. In God's name, surely one of you can tell me what the hell this is.' I started to appreciate how his family had got its surname.

'It's a compass, sir,' came a shaky wee voice from behind me.

Captain Pope was well pleased. 'Correct. It is indeed a compass.' He lifted it up as if he was a mullah displaying the Koran to the faithful. 'There's a small needle in this compass, and it always points in one direction. Can anybody tell me which way the needle always points?'

Well, we were on a roll now, so two-dozen voices piped up, 'North, sir.'

'Correct. It is indeed north. Well done.' He walked over to the board and made a chalk line through the top of the circle and marked it with a large capital 'N'. 'Now,' he said, pointing to the bottom of the circle, 'does anybody know what's opposite to north?'

Oh, this was great, we were beginning to feel like a master class, so everybody shouted at once, 'South, sir.'

He drew a line through the bottom of the circle and marked it with an 'S'.

Things started to get a bit trickier, though, when he pointed to the right of the circle. 'Does anybody know what this direction's called?'

If Steevie had been there, he would have said, 'It's called "right", chief,' but fortunately he wasn't, and a former Boy Scout offered, 'East, sir.'

'Correct. It is indeed east, and opposite east is?'

Same Boy Scout: 'West, sir.'

'Correct. It is indeed west.' So now Captain Pope had marked the four principal points of the compass on his circle on the blackboard.

For the rest of the two-hour lesson he continued to add more compass points to his chalk circle, gradually filling the board with marks and initials, and slowly losing even the Boy Scout in his audience. Finally, he drifted into a wee world of his own, writing ever more chalk marks on his circle without reference to us any more until, by the end of the session, he was pointing at the marks round his chalk compass, while we all had to chant 'North, north-north-east, north-east, east-north-east, east' and so on round every point on his diagram. In fact, he even taught us to pronounce the words as if we were ancient mariners, so we all ended up shouting in unison, 'North, nor-nor-east, nor-east,' and, 'South, sow-sow-west, sow-west.' The fact that none of us had actually been shown a map or held a compass didn't seem to disturb Captain Pope at all.

Day Three, 0800 Hours: 'Whit a Total Waste o' Time.'

Everybody piled into the back of the big army truck and the sergeant closed the canvas flap. There were thirty-two of us – two squads from Perth and our lads from Dundee, although the Perth contingent also supplied the sergeant, a corporal and a captain. The sergeant and the corporal were about sixteen or seventeen, and I recognised the corporal from the drinking episode on the train, but the officer they had given us was at least fifty years old and weighed in at about twenty stone; he was so out of condition that he had to be helped into the front seat of the lorry. As we sped along in the semi-darkness of our canvas cocoon, the young sergeant set out the scenario for us.

'Listen closely, men,' he said, voice quivering with adrenaline. 'We're an elite unit on a special mission behind enemy lines. Oor ronerdezvous wi' oor pick-up team huz been abortid, an' we hae tae mak' oor own way back tae base withoot bein' capchured. We dinna ken exackly where we are an' we canna approach ony civilians fur help. A' we hae is this map' – which he held aloft in the gloom – 'an' this compass' – which he held up next to it. 'Ony questions?' After half a second's pause: 'Richt, then, men, let's git organised.'

Each 'man' was equipped with a First World War vintage .303 calibre Lee Enfield rifle and a five-round clip of blank ammunition. The rifle was almost as big as most of the cadets, so each wee person struggled out from the back of the truck, weighed down with a huge rifle, ammunition pouches, water bottle and haversack full of spare socks and the cheese-and-ham sandwiches that had been handed out at the door of the cookhouse. I didn't feel the slightest bit like part of an elite unit on a special mission behind enemy lines. I felt like a pit pony.

The drab-green truck did an eleven-point turn and disappeared into the morning mist, while the sergeant began organising an all-round defence perimeter along the edges of the narrow country lane. The captain waddled over to the side of the road, rested his enormous arse on the grass bank, lit a fag, and pretended to be casting a professional soldierly eye over the proceedings. Our sergeant and his corporal each carried a Bren – probably one of the best section machine guns ever used by the British Army – and set their weapons up in textbook positions to provide maximum protective fire for our little group. The sergeant and corporal lay in the classic prone position, looking through the sights of their machine guns, covering opposite directions along the road, while the captain finished his fag and the rest of us lay in the ditch beside our antique rifles, picking our noses and eating our sandwiches.

The captain flicked his butt cigarette into the wet grass, convinced himself that the NCOs had adequately performed their duty, then announced that it was time for us to move out. We formed into three ranks and set off down the road with our enormous heavy rifles over our shoulders. The fat captain strode out in front, the corporal kept station in the first rank, and the sergeant marched along at the side of the column calling out the step for our crunching boots every few hundred yards, extolling us to 'Stay alert, men.' The boy really believed all this.

'Ah thought we wiz meant tae be on a secret mission,' the lad next to me whispered to no one in particular. 'Marchin' straight doon the middle o' the road is the maist obvious way o' gettin' capchured, is it no'?'

'No talkin' in the ranks,' shouted the sergeant, but the seeds of doubt had already grown roots.

'Whit aboot no' kennin' whar we are an' no' bein'

able tae ask civilians fur help?' said another little voice. 'There's a sign ower there sayin', "Three miles tae Elgin." This is shite.'

'SILENCE IN THE RANKS!'

We marched secretly down the middle of the road until we could make out the first houses on the fringes of the town. Then suddenly our leader addressed us directly for the first time: 'THE PLATOON WILL SING.'

The only sound that followed his command was the marching of thirty-five pairs of elite hobnail boots and a small bird twittering in a gorse bush.

'SING, YE WEE BASTARDS!' roared the captain. 'YE'RE MEANT TAE BE ENJOYIN' YERSEL'S.' He then began to belt out 'It's a Long Way to Tipperary'.

Twenty-five choruses later, we handed our rifles and blank ammunition in to a real sergeant in the armoury.

'Whit the fuck wiz a' that aboot?' somebody asked the boy sergeant when we got back outside.

Before he had time to dream up a sensible reply 'Whit a total waste o' time' came from a wee lad who was no more than four foot ten and looked completely done in. 'Cerryin' a great big heavy gun aboot fur miles.'

This gave our dedicated sergeant just enough thinking time. 'First, son, it's no' a gun; it's a rifle.' His face then took on a wise, conspiratorial look, and he touched the side of his nose with his index finger, saying to the wee lad in a low voice, 'Second, we wiz probably a divershunury taktic.'

'Whit a load o' shite' floated from an unknown source at the back of the troop.

Day Four, 1200 Hours: Let's Do Lunch

'Hi, pal, how's it goin'?' The guy slopped his plate of grey mince, brown tatties, bright-green peas and mug of tarry tea on to the canteen table, then plopped himself down on the bench beside me.

As I half turned towards my new lunch companion with the standard reply 'No' bad, mate. An' yersel'?' I was confronted with an apparition that confirmed every word of Charlie Darwin's postulations on the origin of species. This lad looked like the result of a mating between a sub-family of South American primates that hadn't been catalogued yet and Smiffy from the Bash Street Kids in *The Beano*. He had buck teeth, no chin, a forehead to die for, hairy hands, and the frayed collar of his battledress tunic came up to about an inch below his frayed lower lip, just like Smiffy's rollneck jersey in the comic strip. He sported a tattoo on his left forearm that stuck out below the rolled-up sleeve of his tunic, confirming that he had been made in Scotland, and he offered the world a manic half-smile below unnaturally big eyes that seemed to look everywhere at once while seeing nothing.

Fuckin' hell, I thought, this boy's a class one nutter.

Now, we all know that the first thing that comes into one's mind when one finds oneself having lunch next to a complete bampot is, 'How in God's name can I get myself out of this shit without setting off this headcase, because these kinds of loonies are always on a hair trigger and awful strong.' That's exactly what my mind was trying to resolve when my lunch companion upped the stakes by delivering his opening gambit through a mouthful of tatties and mince: 'Ah could hae been a astrinut, ye ken.'

Oh, please, God, no, I silently prayed. Dinna send me walkin' through the Valley o' the Shadow o' the Clinically Daft.

Red danger lights started flashing in my head, battle-stations claxons began sounding in my ears, and my left hand tightened round the handle of my fork. I had visions of me and Nutter thrashing about on the canteen floor covered in mince, tatties and tea, while he ripped chunks out of my ear with his teeth and I jabbed my fork ineffectively into his bum.

Luckily, fear hadn't anesthetised my brain completely, so I managed to whimper, 'An astronaut, eh? That's fantastic. But ye hae tae be pretty special tae be ane o' them. So how come ye think ye could hae been an astronaut?'

Nutter glared at this irritating wee moron through his unnaturally large eyes, and I could feel my bowels moving to 'prepare for evacuation' status as I whined, 'Tell me, pal, how could ye hae gone intae the space programme?'

'Ah've nae fear o' heights! Ah could go up the biggest ledders an' scaffulds, as high as ye like, an' Ah nivir get seek.'

Sanity was now accelerating up a Nevada Desert highway, leaving me and Nutter stranded alone among the cactii and tumbleweeds at the side of the road. I realised that my only hope lay in playing along with this ludicrous fantasy, so I said, 'Dinna tak' offence, pal, but a'body gets seek when they're up high. Are ye really tellin' me that ye dinna get a wee bit seek, even when ye're way up in the air?'

I knew that our relationship had moved a couple of points up the good-friends scale when he leaned back, took a huge slavering wet slurp of his tea, looked at me with undisguised pride, and declared, 'No' even the slightest wee bit.'

So far so good: he was still calm and I was still conscious, so I decided to chance my mitt in the interests of fostering relationships between our two planets, while protecting my little delicate body from great harm. Mustering up as much awe and admiration as was credible, I fawned, 'D'ye no' even get dizzy?'

My new astronaut friend was obviously well pleased now, and his body language issued a challenge to any male baboons who may have been lunching in the canteen at the time. 'Never once, pal. Ah think it's jist a gift Ah've got.'

We were now best friends, so when he furtively looked round to see that no one was listening and leaned into me, I was expecting to be invited to be godfather to any future offspring he might sire. It came as a bit of a surprise when he whispered, 'Trooth is, pal, Ah'm no' very good at science things, an' Ah ken they dinna use ledders an' scaffulds fur trainin' astrinuts at Cape Carnarverul, but Ah could easy learn the science things that ye need, an' easy pass a' the tests fur no' gettin' seek, if only Ah ivir got the chance.'

I stared at Nutter for a few moments. I didn't feel threatened any more, just a little bit of empathy with a stranger who had taken me into his trust and who would never realise his dream of doing 'science things' at 'Cape Carnarverul' or anywhere else.

Then he pulled away and took another shovelful of mince. 'Whit's yer name, onyway, buddy?' he sprayed.

'Tam,' I said. 'Tam Broon.'

Day Five, 2015 Hours: Welcome to the World
of the Grown-Ups

One evening after teatime, me and Gordon were sitting on the grass across from the barracks, bulling up our boots, when Captain McClelland came across and sat down beside us. He asked us if we were enjoying the camp and the food, and commented on some other trivia about the final falling-out parade, so we played along by replying that the camp was great and the food was pretty good as well, while wondering what the fuck was going on. Eventually, he steered the conversation round to what he really wanted to talk about, which was what we would do when we left school.

'Dunno, sir,' says Gordon. 'Ah'm no' bad at Inglish, so Ah might see if Ah could get a joab as a jurnilist wi' D. C. Thomson. Ah'd like that a lot, but Ah dunno, though.'

Mr McClelland, for he'd stopped being a captain for just now, nodded slowly and turned to me. 'Whit aboot you, Robertson? Ony ideas?'

I paused for a couple of moments. 'I like art, sir, an' Ah get good marks, so Ah might try tae get intae art skael.'

He nodded slowly again, as if he was looking for flaws in our reasoning and, finding none, carried on. 'Well, it's good that ye've baith clearly gien yer future some thought, but . . .' pause as if he'd just had a brainwave '. . . hae ye ivir considered a career in the army?'

Neither Gordon nor I moved or spoke, and I hoped that he was as proud of me as I was of him, because I knew that we had both just managed to control our instinctive reaction to either laugh or blurt out, 'No way, dumplin'. This camp's good fun fur a week, but ye'd hae tae be daft tae want tae do it a' the time. Plus, people could shoot ye.' But we had far too much respect for Ian McClelland and regard for our own physical well-being to play at smart-arses, so we both tried to look as if the thought had never occurred to us, but hey, now that you mention it, this might be worth considering, right enough.

So we entered a phase in our little discussion where Gordon and me felt obliged to ask him about the great opportunities that the army could provide for guys like us and he enthused about getting a worthwhile trade or even going on to become a junior officer. We soon got bored with this drivel, of course, and began to try to get him to talk about his own military experiences, particularly during the war. We were hoping that he would regale us with tales of adventure and glory, and how our brave kilted lads had won through against all the odds, but the more we pressed in this direction, the more he talked about the laughs he'd had with his mates and the far-flung places he'd seen, and how the army had made him who he was today. Well, this was no use at all. We wanted him to tell us about how he had taken out Jerry machine-gun nests with hand grenades and mown down lines of charging fanatical Nazi stormtroopers like in the *Hotspur* comic.

Our appetite for gory detail became more and more voracious, till I foolishly said, 'It must be really great gettin' the chance tae fight fur yer country. Go on, sir, tell us whit it's really like when ye're in a battle.'

He looked at me for ages before he spoke. 'Let me tell ye a wee story, Wullie.'

It was the first and only time I ever heard him calling a boy by his first name, and Gordon and me were shocked into silence. He sat beside us on the grass and began to tell us about a guy he had first met at a parachute training camp in Buddon Ness, near Dundee. The guy's name was Michael Brannan, an Irish lad who lived in Greenock, and it seemed that he and Ian clicked right away and became firm friends. Evidently, Michael had been given more than his share of the gift of the blarney and he kept the ladies, landlords and citizens of war-weary Britain entertained on many an evening in blacked-out pubs beside windswept army bases. For almost the next eighteen months Michael Brannan and Ian McClelland shared fun, hardships, girlfriends and cigarettes as they were moved from camp to camp while the Allied forces prepared for, and then executed, the invasion of

Normandy. According to McClelland, Michael then kept the ladies, landlords and citizens of war-weary Europe entertained on many an evening in bombed-out pubs in the ravaged towns and villages that they had both helped to liberate.

Less than three months before the war ended, McClelland and Michael were part of a platoon walking in single file down a pavement in a small town in northern Germany where their unit was mopping up resistance. They were all keeping close into the shadows of the buildings as they moved along, and although still watchful for booby traps on the ground and snipers in upper-floor windows, everybody knew that it was really all over: the enemy was beaten and soon everybody would be heading home to a hero's welcome and unlimited kisses and fish suppers. Suddenly, a uniformed figure stepped out from a doorway about twenty yards ahead and fired a burst of machine-gun rounds at the line of men on the pavement. Michael buckled on to the road screaming and clutching his right thigh, while McClelland instinctively dropped on to one knee and shot the figure through the chest. Several others in the section joined in and riddled the prone soldier's body until there could be no possibility of further threat.

Gordon and me looked sideways at each other, while McClelland just sat there looking straight ahead. Although this was more like what we had thought we wanted – a heroic British para drilling the sneaky Jerry who shot his pal – the immediacy of the action and the tone of McClelland's voice were starting to make us feel not quite right about this. I couldn't believe that he was speaking to us in this way: it was totally out of character and I had the distinct feeling of being a spectator among the mob around the guillotine.

He quietly carried on, 'Ah got over tae Michael tae see how bad he'd been hit. He'd a severe wound in his upper right thigh an' a flesh wound in his right forearm, but his life wasnae in danger an' the medics were quick on the scene wi' needles an' drips tae stabilise him an' get him ready fur evacuation.'

He told us that after they stretchered Michael away and everybody was satisfied that the area was secure, the patrol set off again down the pavement, and as he came level with the soldier he had just killed, he looked down at the body. I detected the very slightest tremor in his PE-instructor voice as he told us, 'He was a laddie o' aboot fifteen or sixteen, not much aulder than the twa o' you. His tunic was far too big fur him, an' the sleeves almost covered his hands as he lay there lifeless. That's whit it's *really* like fighting fur yer country, lads, an' Ah pray tae God that ye'll never get the chance.'

In that moment I realised why Ian McClelland spent so many hours organising weekend football and rugby teams and helping boys to fulfil their potential as athletes, sportsmen, swimmers, teachers or even junior officers. True, he was a natural teacher and a man who genuinely wanted to keep kids on the straight and narrow, but I was convinced that, in some small way, he was also still trying to make his peace with one little brainwashed soul who gave up his life for his *Führer* and his Reich.

That night after lights-out, I lay in my bunk in the dark with my eyes stinging and my throat raw, thinking about the poor wee German laddie who, but for the hand of Fate, could easily have been me. But mostly I was realising the pain that I now knew was still carried by Captain Ian McClelland, inspirational teacher, secret carer and hard man of this parish. Neither Gordon nor I ever spoke about the episode again, and I went right off buying the *Hotspur*.

Day Six, 0930 Hours: The Grand Parade

The day we said goodbye to the Elgin Barracks and got the train back to bonny Dundee, we were told that because we had all done so well, we would be granted the special honour of being included in a formal inspection of the whole battalion by the camp's commanding officer, a lieutenant colonel with a distinguished military career and two second names, with a hyphen. This was a real privilege. We were the second battalion the Black Watch Army Cadet Force, and wore a little square of regimental tartan on our shoulder and the regiment's badge on our blue bonnets with the distinctive red hackle. The most exciting thing for us was that it wouldn't be just a bunch of Dundee scuffs on the parade ground. The Territorial Army and, most impressive of all, the Regular Army had units from the Second Battalion of the Black Watch stationed in this very same camp, and we were going to be standing in line with real soldiers and inspected by a genuine high-ranking officer. So the night before the parade, each boy in the barrack hut spent hours polishing and cleaning every item of kit that he would be wearing the next morning, till every piece of brass shone like gold and every toecap on every boot reflected the shining brass like a black mirror.

The grand moment arrived. The rest of the Second Battalion of the Black Watch Army Cadets and me stood in shining ranks on one side of the parade ground, while the TA and the regulars took up position on the other two sides of the square. After several minutes standing motionless 'at ease', the lieutenant colonel sauntered on to the parade ground, closely followed by an apparition that struck terror into the hearts of all the boy soldiers in Elgin and would have persuaded wog tribesmen in Afghanistan to instantly flee back into the hills. The CO's shadow and protector was Regimental Sergeant Major McLeod, whom God had created for the express purpose of serving in the Black Watch. He was about six foot two, ramrod straight and carrying a polished hardwood stick with a gleaming brass top under his armpit. He looked awesome, beautiful and terrifying as he marched into the middle of the parade ground behind his commander, his Black Watch kilt and regimental sporran swaying with each stride, and his whole demeanour giving voice to the regimental motto '*Nemo me impune lacessit*', which I had already been told meant 'No one assails me with impunity' or, more colloquially, 'Naebody fucks aboot wi' me an' gets awa' wi' it': pretty much the same sentiment. Our commanding officer stopped in the middle of the parade ground and RSM McLeod came to a crashing halt two paces behind him.

Even from this distance I could see that Regimental Sergeant Major McLeod was surveying the cadet contingent as if he thought we were an ill-disciplined, disrespectful, Communist rabble of young tearaways who needed some old-fashioned discipline to whip us into shape. After a few moments, the lieutenant colonel spoke a couple of words to his RSM, who took two crisp paces forward, smashed his feet together, looked over all of us as if we were some rare species of vermin, then proclaimed in a voice like a low flying aircraft, 'THEEE BATTALIAAAN WILL COME

TOOO ATTENSHUN. BATTAAALIAAAAAAAAN,
ATTEAAAAAN-SHUN!' The actual 'shun' bit sounded
as if had been barked out by a giant German shepherd
with a throat infection, but it sure had the desired
effect. About four hundred right boots crunched into
the parade ground in perfect unison as the entire
battalion – regulars, territorials and cadets – snapped
to attention.

Bloody hell, I thought, we're really good. Surely
even the RSM must be impressed wi' that performance.

Wrong. Nothing impressed McLeod, least of all us.
He'd been there, seen it, done it, shagged it if it was
friendly, shot it if it was hostile, and then declined the
offer of a T-shirt. To him, we were still an ill-
disciplined, disrespectful, Communist rabble.

So the grand inspection began. Our commanding
officer and his Rottweiler RSM marched across the
parade ground directly towards us, which came as a bit
of a surprise, since I had assumed that they would be
doing a real inspection with the proper army first,
before having a token walk around the lines of the boy
soldiers, smiling and nodding here and there, then
back to the mess for a gin-and-tonic.

Oh, aye, I thought. This is jist so that we'll mak' the
rest o' the parade look good.

The lieutenant colonel started to walk down the
front rank of his boy army, occasionally stopping to

exchange pleasantries so that he could pretend that he was interested. Two paces behind him came RSM McLeod, who didn't even try to pretend that he was interested, and glared across the ranks of boy soldiers and at the back of his CO's head with equal disdain. I was standing in the front rank, so the exchanges between the CO and the cadets that he chose to speak to became more and more audible as he moved up the ranks towards me. Finally, he stopped in front of a little person standing two down from me. This wee guy looked like a child scarecrow dressed in a grown-up's army uniform: spiky ginger hair stuck out from below either side of his crumpled blue bonnet, and his creased uniform hung off his skinny frame like he'd just been liberated from a Japanese prisoner-of-war camp in Borneo.

The CO blinked at him and went through the motions. 'Arr you enjowing youwsewf at the ceamp, Pwivate?'

'Sure am, Lootenint,' says the little lad.

Regimental Sergeant Major McLeod visibly winced, and there was a long pause while the lieutenant colonel took in what had been said to him.

'And . . . eh . . . how . . . how long exactwy have you ectuawwy been in the awmy cadets?'

'Comin' up fur three weeks, Lootenint.' The boy was really beginning to enjoy this military banter.

The camp's commanding officer looked at him as if

he had just arrived from the jungles of Sumatra with a bone through his nose to take up post on the floor of the London Stock Exchange.

'Jowwy good. Jowwy good indeed. Well, cawwy on, Pwivate.' He then smiled weakly at the wee figure with barely disguised revulsion and moved on down the ranks, while the poor little lad beamed and thought he was the bee's knees, having engaged the nice 'lootenint' in such an interesting conversation.

His brief dream was shattered when Sergeant Major McLeod's nose suddenly appeared about two inches from his own, and a sound like a cornered tiger snarled into his face, 'Hoooo the fuck d'yooo think y'arrr? John fuckin' Wayne?'

The laddie was transformed from beaming self-confidence to a quivering, incontinent wreck, and at that moment nobody on the planet looked less like John fucking Wayne.

Chapter Eleven

A New Experience
Every Day

Just another day at the office.

A single pint of milk doesn't weigh that much, but after an hour of jogging up four flights of tenement stairs with a carrier of eight pints in each hand, you begin to feel an ache in your shoulders and neck, and by the end of a three-hour shift, the ache has spread right down your arms and over your back. On a bright, warm morning in mid-July, it was easy to forget sore muscles and to take a few seconds to realise that the rising sun made the tenement look as though it had been roofed with burnished-bronze slates.

In summer, sandshoes and T-shirts and flying up and down stairs and taking shortcuts through the backs of pre-fabs made it all seem like a big game. Avril had even devised little competitions over the years to make it more fun for her laddies, and, incidentally, to make sure we ran ourselves ragged for the efficiency of the business. Two boys would drop off with a full crate and two empty carriers each to deliver for a whole cul-de-sac, while the lorry screeched away to another part of the round. It was a big thing to be the one standing beside the empty crate when Auld Jim swung back round the corner, so each competitor pounded up and down paths and vaulted over wee walls to fulfil his quota first. It was even better if you could be sitting on the crate while the other lad wasn't even in sight: that drew a huge roar from the returning milk laddies on the step and a great big grin from Avril. The same daft games were played out running up closes, collecting milk money or unloading the crates at the end of the shift, and in the warmth of a July sunrise it was great fun.

In the middle of winter, however, it was very different. Gone were the sandshoes and T-shirts; in their place were thick jeans, heavy jumpers, jerkins, wellies and woolly hats, and frozen fingers. You could put on thick socks to keep your toes warm or a knitted balaclava to keep your lugs cosy, but you couldn't carry four empties in each hand with gloves on, so every winter morning our hands and fingers froze through pain to numbness. Each laddie had a pair of knitted woollen gloves from his grannie deep in the pocket of his jerkin, and pulled them over his freezing blue hands as soon as he was back at the huddin' rail. It didn't make the slightest bit of difference, though, because no sooner were you on than Avril pushed a couple of full carriers in front of you and the lads on either side gripped your shoulders so you could whip off the gloves, grab the handles of the carriers, step backwards, and get delivering again.

Scottish winter mornings are pitch dark, and every close seemed to beckon me and my carriers into its cold, black, yawning mouth. It was even worse if there was a stair light on, because the only one that ever worked was inevitably right at the top floor and cast an eerie glow down to the stairwell four floors below, so that by the time the yellow light bathed the ground-floor stairs, they looked like the perfect ambush site for lurking Count Dracula and a couple of his white-faced mates. I could almost see their bloodshot eyes following me as they hunched deep in the shadows and adjusted their bowties. So whenever possible, I clutched an empty bottle in my right hand, ready to defend myself against agents of the Prince of Darkness or drunk men lying on the stairs. At least once a week I took an almighty swing with my bottle at some non-existent spectre up a close or a poor randy tom cat out on the prowl behind somebody's garden shed.

They say that soldiers at war endure endless hours of dull routine punctuated by moments of frenzied activity; well, this is just how it was for milk laddies. I'd learned my round so well that I could, and often did, do it in my sleep. Every morning we trotted up the same paths and closes carrying our wire carriers stacked with full pint bottles; then we trotted back down again with our hands or our carriers filled with the jingling empty glass residue of yesterday's delivery. When I was alone up a tenement stair or jumping over a fence into somebody's front garden to get to my next delivery, I just mentally shut down and motored on to get that bit of the round finished. My body was mechanically providing McNab (no tipper) with her one pint a day and the Frazers (thruppenny tippers) with their two pints except on Sunday, but my mind was far, far away from the sleet or the rain running down my neck or the bleach-smelling close stairs or the front paths of the pre-fabs that seemed to be specifically designed to accommodate a thin film of ice.

Like the wartime soldiers, we all just got on with the humdrum and relied on occasional ludicrous happenings and each other to keep going. Tiny little things like eating our stolen rolls with a thick layer of raspberry jam on the back of the speeding truck gave a huge boost to our morale, even if the roll was soggy with morning drizzle. Even our 'opposition' helped. There was only one point on the whole round where we came into direct eye contact with other milk laddies. We never really thought of newspaper delivery lads and lassies as being part of 'us', because they didn't get up till we were nearly finished our round. Roll-delivery boys were just as bad: only worth having because they could provide milk laddies with illicit breakfasts. But we had a genuine affinity with the lads hanging off the back of the lorry that zipped past us in the opposite direction along Strathmore Avenue at a quarter past six. They were just the same as us in a differently liveried 'larry'.

If both lorries were smack on schedule, we'd cross exactly outside the wee fire station at a combined speed of about eighty miles an hour. Every second that either truck was behind target meant about twenty yards lost, so the crew went into raptures of catcalling and obscene gestures if we passed them three or four hundred yards down from the fire station, sometimes even further if their truck had encountered an unforeseen problem, like some plonker falling off the step. Of course, they did exactly the same to us, and it would be our turn to look the other way or light a fag. Maybe there was a secret pact between Avril and the guy on the other lorry to take it in turns to lose, so their pack of wee boys would pull the sledge even harder.

But every now and again, somebody would innocently do something or say something that had everybody laughing through the rest of the shift, and even more occasionally, something would happen that had us chuckling for the rest of the week.

Fat Boab seemed to be getting fatter in front of our eyes, and he knew it. He was slowing down and the effort of running his round was beginning to tell on his overburdened knees and lungs, although he tried desperately to keep up with the pack. One beautiful crisp, clear January morning, the chains on the lorry's wheels churned through the hard-packed snow along Gardener Street, which was at least a straight half-mile long, with tenements on one side and a huge area of allotments on the other, which is probably how it got its name. The allotments usually looked like an Albanian refugee settlement, with old chairs, prams, bits of wire mesh and an occasional cabbage, but today it looked like an Austrian Alpine ski resort, with millions of minute sparkling diamonds glistening on the surface of the snow that smoothed everything like a deep covering of pure-white custard.

Suddenly, Johnny stepped back off the lorry but kept hold of the huddin' rail. Jim was only going about fifteen miles an hour, but Johnny's feet skimmed along the surface of the hard snow like a downhill ski champion. We all whooped with delight and leaped off the back so we could go skiing as well and soon everybody was being dragged along, leaving a fine mist of snow and ice in our wake. Everybody except Boab. You could see that he really wanted to be like the rest of us, but he was obviously scared shitless at the prospect of being pulled along a snow-covered road behind the churning wheels of a loaded milk lorry.

'C'mon, Boab, it's great. It's nae effurt at a'.'

'Ye'll mak' it easy, Boab. Jist step doon!'

'Go on, Boab, ye're missin' oot.'

Eventually, Fat Boab closed his eyes and stepped backwards into the abyss.

When Boab opened his eyes, he was a skier. He stood with the rest of us, hands on the rail and shoes gliding over the hard snow. We were all laughing and whooping and looking at the painfully white snow piled up over the greenhouses as the allotments whizzed past; this was as good as the rich fowk got on their holiday to the Alps. Steevie began to sing some nonsense that he thought was Austrian and soon we were all singing and yodelling at the top of our voices. We were as happy as any millionaire on the slopes of Val d'Isère. Johnny was posing like an international playboy, Si was working out the co-efficient of linear frictional resistance of the snow or something, Steevie was trying to ski on one leg, and Fat Boab was beaming and singing and moving his bulk with amazing dexterity to negotiate small bumps in the road.

Then I saw the slightest of movements out the

corner of my eye and in an instant Fat Boab had vanished. As one, we all looked back and saw Boab lying in the middle of the road as if he'd been poleaxed. Avril saw it too and banged an empty bottle on the floor of the lorry. Within moments we were all back on the step and banging furiously for Auld Jim to stop. It took about a hundred yards for Jim to bring the lorry to a controlled stop on the snow. Gordon, Wee John and I leaped off the step and went tearing back up the road to the motionless chubby body. His nose was bleeding badly, and he had scraped the skin off one side of his face. We turned him over and did our impersonation of people who know what they're doing with injured people, but it was obvious, even to us, that nothing was broken and he wasn't severely hurt. His worst injuries were his jeans, which were ripped beyond repair, and a Cadbury's Flake, which was mashed beyond redemption.

'Whit the fuck happened?'

Wee Good John had spotted exactly what had happened and pointed back up the road. 'He hit that drain cover. It's got nae sna' on it, look.'

Sure enough, an iron manhole cover stood out stark and black against the white snow, right in the centre of the road. Obviously, people in the tenements were waking up and having baths or pouring hot water down the sink, gradually melting the snow on the manhole cover above the communal drain. Two parallel lines about four inches apart showed how good a skier Fat Boab was, until these parallel lines reached the manhole cover. After that point the snow was pitted with evidence of flailing limbs, torn jeans, blood and bits of Flake. The rest of us shared out Boab's deliveries as he sat nursing his wounded knees and wounded pride on the floor of the truck. 'And the winner of this year's men's Olympic downhill slalom with manholes, representing Scotland, is Robert Findlay from Dundee.' Hooray.

I think that was the final lesson that Boab needed, because the next morning he announced he was going to tell Avril that he was leaving. 'It's jist tae much fur me now, lads. Ye kin see Ah'm strugglin'.' He was right: we could see he wasn't having a good time, no matter how much we tried to cover for him on the more exerting bits of his round, so after some half-hearted attempts to persuade him to stay, he gave in his two weeks' notice. Avril accepted right away.

Fat Boab's replacement duly turned up at five to five on the following Monday morning, and Avril took him aside for the usual wee pep talk before bringing him over to where we were all lounging around the loaded truck, impatient to go. He looked like any other fresh-faced fourteen-year-old and I figured him to be in the year below us at school.

'This is Frank,' said Avril. 'He's takin' ower Boab's roond.'

'Hi, Frank.' Boab was, rightly, the first to greet the new laddie and we all joined in the welcome, while making a space on the back step for him to get his first introduction to the huddin' rail.

Frank had no sooner gripped the rail than Auld Jim gunned the heavily laden lorry out of the depot for our new recruit's first sight of the round. The lad looked like I must have looked on my first day – exhilarated, excited and just a little bit overawed – but he kept it together as Avril sat wedged between the crates, giving him the instructions that would preserve his life, and the skin on his knees.

Fat Boab introduced us all in turn, and we smiled or nodded as he gave our name, but this wasn't enough for Wee Good. 'Ah've nivir met onybody ca'd Frank afore.' He beamed as though this should be taken as a great compliment.

'It's short fur Francis,' the new lad replied, beginning the revelations.

'Ah canna mind seein' ye at the skael, Frank,' said Gordon, making conversation. 'Whit year are ye in?'

'Ah'm in third year, but Ah'm no' at Kirkton – Ah'm at the Johnnies'.'

'Oh, so ye're a Pape, then?' Steevie broke the silence as subtly as always.

'Aye, Ah'm Catholic. How, is that a problem fur ye?' Frank had the look of a young man who was no stranger to religious bigotry.

'Not at all,' Gordon piped. 'It's jist that Steevie here's always wanted tae learn the words o' "Hail Mary", eh, Steevie?'

Steevie put on a mock pained expression. 'Ah've only got the one problem roond here, Frank – that daft bastard ower there.' He flicked his thumb contemptuously at Gordon.

We all chuckled, the sectarian divide was bridged, and Frank settled in as a full member of the tight little band.

For the next two weeks, Fat Boab showed Frank his round and all the tricks of the trade to shouts of 'Dinna dae it like him, Frank – ye're supposed tae run' and 'Jist 'cos Boab pechs an' bla's a' the time disnae mean ye hae tae.' But when Fat Boab Findlay's last day arrived, it was like one of my own family was going away. We all mumbled things like, 'See ye at skael, then, pal,' when we really wanted to tell him how much we would miss his presence on the lorry. Good old Johnny closed it by summing up the emotion we all felt: 'There'll be room on the step fur anithir three laddies now, Boab.'

Of all of us, Johnny took longest to accept Frank. After all, here was a new young male in his prime joining the pack, and this might well pose a threat to Johnny's alpha-male status, so cool Johnny played it friendly but guarded. The test happened four or five days after Boab had left, and Frank was running deliveries with only occasional reminders from Avril. We were rattling up the Kingsway at the end of the round and Johnny decided he needed a well-earned fag, so he expertly pulled his packet of ten Embassy from his breast pocket, flicked the top open with one hand, and pulled one out with his lips: even taking a cigarette was an opportunity for a pose. For the last five minutes, though, he had been lovingly caressing his semi with his right hand in his trouser pocket. He was so fond of this pastime that he had worn a big hole in his pocket and was able to get straight to the object of his affection without any material barrier. By this time, he had finally managed to wiggle the whole length of his semi through the hole so that it completely filled his pocket.

Frank was standing next to him on the step and Johnny made a big show of keeping his right hand securely on the huddin' rail while he sorted out his fag with his left. 'Get ma lighter oot ma pockit fur me, wid ye, Frank?' says Johnny, pushing his right hip slightly towards the lad.

'Aye, nae bother,' replied Frank, and obligingly thrust his hand into Johnny's pocket.

I suppose it took about a second for Frank's brain to work out that cigarette lighters are cold, metallic and solid, and what he had in his hand was warm, fleshy and semi-pliable. About half a second later, his brain started to shriek the awful realisation that his fingers were in fact round a partially erect human penis. The lad's arm jerked back above his head as if he had touched a naked flame. 'Ye dirty bastard!' he screamed, trying to wipe his hand on his shirt.

Johnny was speaking through sobs of laughter. 'Oh, Frankie baby,' he moaned. 'That wiz so great.'

Slowly the rest of us began to twig what had happened and tried to suppress our own hysterics as we attempted to console Frank, who was thrashing about, wiping his fingers on everything around him.

'He really is a dirty bastard. Ye should hae skwashed his ba's,' was the only meaningful contribution I could think of.

But the test had been passed, and even Frank eventually began to smile. 'Ye're fuckin' mental, ye pervert.'

'This'll mean twenty-sivin "Hail Marys" fur you, boy,' Gordon offered helpfully. '"Bless me, Father, for I have rubbed another lad's knob."'

As it turned out, though, Frank wasn't the only one who should have been seeking absolution that night for sins of the flesh.

Avril paid us after the Friday-night milk-money collection, and Gordon, Steevie and I always walked home together, pockets bulging with pennies, thrup-pennies, sixpences, shillings and every other denomin-ation of British legal tender. As we were getting near home one Friday evening, flush with wages and tips, we heard a great shouting and crashing and swearing coming from outside the entrance to the Silver Birch. Obviously, a fight was in progress, so the three of us sprinted up to the end of the road to watch the cabaret. We weren't disappointed when we turned the corner. Two police cars were in the middle of the road with doors open and blue lights flashing, while a police van had backed up on the pavement in front of the door to the pub. Four cops were trying to control the hyena pack surrounding the scene, while another four were doing their best to separate two gladiators and get them into the back of the van.

The three of us joined the crowd just as the first guy was being bundled inside the van and the rain started, so we sarcastically clapped and jeered the efforts of the cops, pulled our jacket collars up round our ears, and settled down to enjoy the rest of the show. We were behind several other people and couldn't see too clearly, but we could make out two policemen who had the second guy down on the paving slabs trying to get handcuffs on him. It was obvious that this bloke had no intention of surrendering peacefully, so we jockeyed for the best position to watch him take down a few of the Sheriff of Nottingham's men before he was overpowered. The bloke put up a noble struggle, but the two constables who had managed to get the first guy into the back of the van joined the fray and soon it was all over: the guy was pinned, handcuffed, pulled to his feet, and dragged towards the police van. It was raining quite heavily now and the crowd had started to disperse, so we had an unrestricted view of this wild-eyed bloke, his hair wet with rain and blood, being frogmarched into the van. I suddenly jerked backwards like I'd been jabbed with an electric cattle prod. It was Steevie's dad.

Steevie stood there with rain dripping off the end of his nose looking at his dad being pushed into the van.

'Come on, Steevie, let's go,' said Gordon. 'Ye'll hae tae get hame an' tell yer muthir whit's happened.'

Steevie just stood there silent as the doors were slammed and the van drove away. His face was set hard and he was biting his lip, deeply humiliated by what his friends and neighbours had seen.

'Nae problem, Steevie,' I said. 'The bastard must hae deserved it or yer dad wouldnae hae whacked him.'

Steevie just put his hands into his pockets and set off towards his house at a fast walk. After about ten yards, he broke into a run.

Gordon and me went back to my house and sat on the bed in my room. Each of us avoided mentioning Steevie or his dad, and I tried to lighten things up by putting our latest purchase on the turntable. 'Please Please Me' had been released only a few weeks before, and we lay back on the bed, absently listening to the song again, trying to blot out the memory of what we had just seen, and trying hard to think of something to say that would change the subject. John Lennon was getting to his final plea to his girl to please him when Gordon suddenly said, 'Whit aboot Maureen Duncan, though, Wullie? How wid ye like tae be locked in a shed wi' her fur the night?'

My mind instantly forgot the scenes outside the Birch and I started to imagine being locked in a shed all night with the sexiest girl in the whole school. At fourteen and a half, Maureen Duncan had the body and the mind of a girl of seventeen, and she was every boy's fantasy. I began to remember the sight of her long, blond hair and even longer shapely legs as she sat at the next table in the dinner hall, and could visualise myself touching the firm breasts that tried to push through her tight school blouse.

'Can ye see her wi' nuthin' on, Goardin? Jist think whit it wid be like skweezin' her tits.'

For the next half-hour, Steevie, his dad, the milk round and everything else paled into the distance as Gordon and me lay on my single bed, locked in a shed with Maureen for the whole night.

'Bless me, Father . . .'

Chapter Twelve

The Amazing Power of Sticking Together

'The doctrine of the conditions of the liberation
of the proletariat.'
So Grannie Brannan told me. Good stuff for a
ten-year-old.

Johnny and Steevie were the longest-serving hands
on the lorry, and for months they had been filling
Wee Good John's head with tales about the exploits
of the guy he had replaced. The lad was inexplicably
called 'Bendy', and very slowly, morning after morning, they gradually elevated him into some kind of
super-hero who earned two pounds ten in tips and

could carry six empties in each hand. The rest of us added to the conspiracy by 'oohing' and 'aahing', and demanding ever more flowery details of Bendy's heroic exploits from the two veterans of his time as a milk laddie.

For us, it was just a stupid game, but poor Wee Good sucked it all in like a sponge. I could see that he was gradually being manipulated into comparing himself with the legendary Bendy, and trying to show that he was every bit as good at everything, particularly when it came to working on the lorry and delivering the milk. If Bendy carried three full pints in each hand, Wee Good John tried unsuccessfully to carry four. If Bendy arrived every morning at ten to five to help load the truck, Wee John arrived at a quarter to. Johnny, Steevie and probably the rest of us mercilessly fanned the flames until Bendy was to Wee Good John as Fidel Castro was to John F. Kennedy: an abomination that had to be bettered, no matter what the cost.

Every morning at about ten to eight, the truck roared up Dundee's outer ring road on its way back to the depot, and the harder Auld Jim hit the accelerator, the more we liked it. Each moment saved on the final half-mile journey along that dual carriageway was another moment that we could savour having our bacon and eggs in the kitchen at home before setting off for another day at school. This road, imaginatively called the Kingsway, carried all the traffic that just wanted to get round the city on their way to somewhere else.

It had been built in the 1930s and was conceptually years ahead of its time, with two lanes in each direction, a ten-yard grass central reservation in between, and a cycle path and pavement, separated by a tree-lined verge, along each side. It was the work of a true visionary and a masterpiece of over-engineering for its time. It formed a beautiful, leafy conduit for the handfuls of little Ford, Austin, Standard and Triumph cars that sped efficiently round the city all year long, and in summer it also carried a few BSA motorbikes and lengthy convoys of lorries piled high with punnets of raspberries and strawberries freshly picked from the berry fields that stretched out to the horizon in all directions from the city limits. For 363 days of the year, through each season and all weather, it also carried a flatbed five-ton Bedford truck, stacked up with crates of empty bottles and tired milk laddies on their way back to their depot.

About five hundred yards before the roundabout where we turned off for our imperial state drive through Kirkton, stopping only for me to deliver the final pint of milk to Pat in Fort Apache before swinging into our depot, an iron bridge carried a single-track railway line across the dual carriageway. The big grey girders rested on three stone columns, one at either side of the road and one that grew out of the grass on the central reservation. Four or five times a day a labouring little locomotive belched black smoke across the Kingsway as it ponderously dragged a string of wagons laden with rocks or turnips or some other vital cargo across the narrow structure on its way to God knows where. Steevie had once remarked, 'If we wiz in the Rezintince, we could bla' this bridge up dead easy.' Although everybody earnestly agreed that this was a fair point and turned away trying not to be seen to laugh, Steevie had made a serious observation. It actually did look remarkably like something that John Mills and his heroic mates would be strapping explosives to in the middle of a black-and-white movie.

One morning as we were passing under the bridge, Johnny said offhandedly to Steevie, 'Mind the time that Bendy threw the golf ba'?'

Steevie might have been a bit slow on his feet, but he was fast enough in his head and replied enthusiastically, 'Oh, aye, Johnny, that wiz really somethin' tae see.'

Johnny reeled out a bit more bait. 'Ah really thought he wiz goin' tae dae it. He wiz that close.' He held his thumb and index finger about two inches apart.

The two of them had taken all of us in now, and despite the fact that he must have suspected a major piss-take, Gordon said warily, 'Whit's this aboot a golf ba'? Whit did Bendy dae that wiz so close?'

Johnny kept both hands on the huddin' rail and leaned out backwards over the speeding tarmac below him so he could see past Si and me to look Gordon straight in the eyes. 'It wiz amaizin', Goardin,' he said with awe. 'We wiz comin' up tae that bridge back there one moarnin' when Bendy pulls this golf ba' oot o' his pockit and says he bets us a' that he could throw it ower the bridge an' catch it on the other side efter the larry went under.'

Of course, Gordon and all the rest of us twigged right away, but Wee Good John gazed at Johnny like a child gazes at a department-store Santa.

'So whit did ye say, Johnny?' inquired Gordon earnestly.

'Well, we bet him a shillin' each, like, 'cos we thought that naebody could possibly dae that an' we wiz on a dead-cert winner.'

'So whit happened?'

Steevie took up the story, equally impressed. 'Well, when we wiz comin' up tae the bridge, Bendy asked us tae move alang the step an' gie him room. Then, at the last meenit, he took the golf ba' in his hand an' threw it up ower the bridge.' Wee Good was in a trance by this time. 'We went under the bridge an' when we come oot the other side, a' o' us looked up. The golf ba' hud gone richt ower the bridge an' wiz comin' doon towards the back o' the larry, jist like Bendy had said. He leaned oot tae catch it, but it landed too far back an' he couldna reach far enough – he missed it by nae mair than twa inches.'

We all pretended to be overwhelmed by Bendy's superhuman feat. 'Christ, Steevie, Ah wid nivir hae believed that onybody could dae such a thing. Naebody else could ivir hae a chance o' gettin' even close tae that,' gasped Gordon.

Steevie stood deep in thought, hands wide on the huddin' rail, gazing down at the step and occasionally glancing up at Wee Good, till he eventually murmured, 'Wee John could,' in a tone that was just the right balance of soul-searching insight and grudging respect.

The jaws of the bear trap were now gaping open and primed, ready to snap into the first hapless ankle that triggered its mechanism. Nobody was surprised at the owner of the ankle that immediately hopped tentatively forward on to the spring plate.

Wee John was wary but desperately wanted to square up to the legend of Bendy so that he could destroy the myth and show himself to be just as good, if not better, than his predecessor. 'How come ye think that Ah could dae the same as Bendy, Steevie? Whit mak's ye think that Ah could throw a golf ba' ower the bridge?'

Steevie took centre stage and showed why he should have become an actor or a politician after leaving school. 'Jist look at yersel', John.' He oiled sincerely. 'Ye're wee an' skinny, so that mak's ye lightnin' fest. Yur reeaakshuns is fest as fuck, even fester than Bendy

probarly, so ye could whip oot tae catch a wee ba'
better than ony o' the rest o' us, even better than a wee
shit like me.'

The whole step laughed at Steevie's self-deprecating
joke, but the seeds of events to come had been sown,
watered and fertilised, and all but two of the crew knew
it. Wee Good John didn't know it because he wanted so
much to believe it was all true, and Steevie didn't know
it because he thought that throwing golf balls over
bridges was a stupid waste of effort that didn't make
any money.

As the lorry approached the bridge on the next
couple of trips, we conspired to build up Wee John's
confidence that he could match, indeed even surpass,
Bendy's feat by actually catching the golf ball. By the
third morning, John was subconsciously lining up his
little body on the step, while the truck hurtled towards
the bridge and his eyes darted back and forward
between the girders and the road. All of us quietly
whistled through our teeth as Wee John subtly moved
into his pre-launch stance, and even Si started talking
about 'arcs' and 'trajectories'. Every one of us knew
exactly what we were doing and none of us did a thing
to stop it. It's always puzzled me that one of the
characteristics of bullies is that they very often have a
deep liking for their victim, and so it was with us. We
all liked Wee Good John a whole lot and would have
gone well out of our way to protect him, but we just

allowed the thrill of the big stitch-up to cloud the harsh reality of what we were doing.

So, at seven fifty one crisp, bright morning, Fletcher's milk lorry hammered up the Kingsway as usual, filled with rattling crates of empty milk bottles and knackered milk laddies hanging on the back. The dark grey railway bridge loomed into view, silhouetted against the clear, blue morning sky, and Wee John's face set into a mask of determination as he pulled a golf ball from the pocket of his jeans. He was flanked by Johnny on one side and Si on the other, and their first reaction was to look at each other in smiling amusement. Avril had her back to us, sitting on the floor of the truck and pushing the crates of empty bottles towards the front with her feet, while everyone else gradually became aware of Wee Good leaning dangerously backwards out over the road, his left hand white-knuckled around the huddin' rail and his extended right hand clutching a battered old golf ball. Time slowed down: I was conscious of the bridge advancing towards us in slow motion and of all the other lads staring at John as they waded through treacle trying to get their brains to tell their mouths and limbs to do something.

Wee Good John's moment of glory was doomed to disaster as soon as the golf ball left his fingers in a Herculean attempt to better Bendy. Every laddie on the step watched in horror as the hard wee ball curved through the air without a hope in hell of clearing the bridge, clanged into the grey-blue metal of the lower girders, and shot straight downwards. Auld Jim must have just been nestling into his seat in the cab, drifting into the thankful end of yet another delivery day, when a hundred-miles-an-hour meteorite suddenly smashed into the bonnet of his lorry, ricocheted off his windscreen, and vanished into the rough on the edge of the cycle path. He instinctively ducked and slammed on the brakes and the truck, weighed down with crates, bottles and laddies, skidded and slewed along the carriageway, vomiting crates and milk bottles over five hundred yards of Dundee's ring road, before finally coming to rest at a drunken angle with one wheel on the central reservation and a torn rear offside tyre in the middle of the overtaking lane. It's odd how your brain reacts to these kinds of events, because I just stood there on the step thinking that the view back along the road looked sort of spiritual in the morning light, with wisps of blue smoke from melted tyres rising slowly above broad trails of shimmering smashed glass and twisted metal crates. All too soon, however, the real world slowly returned: the blurred shapes around me formed into milk laddies, and the low buzzing in my ears became words, just like waking up in the dentist's chair when you've had the gas.

Avril was white as a ghost, although she checked that each of her laddies was relatively undamaged before allowing herself to sit, trembling, next to me on the back step. The rest of the crew were going through their own attempts at trauma management. Gordon was tightly gripping my arm and speaking into my buzzing ear at great speed. Frank was ripping open a packet of five Woodbine. Johnny was trying desperately to look as if his pulse rate hadn't altered, while holding his bowels in check. Si was sat on the kerb looking grateful to be alive and gazing back at the bridge trying to calculate the angle at which the golf ball must have hit the bonnet. Steevie looked totally unmoved and sat on the grass with his back against a couple of mangled milk crates, dispassionately surveying the wreckage strewn all over the road while he rolled up another of his horrific mixtures of new tobacco and dog-ends. Wee John was standing forlornly in the middle of the carriageway, on the edge of tears and trying to come to terms with the carnage he had caused.

Auld Jim burst from his cab in a cloud of Johnnie Walker fumes. His hip flask had been punctured, his arse had been lacerated, his lorry had been dented, and several hundred of his bottles had been smashed. As if this wasn't enough, he would probably have 'boabies' knocking at his door later in the day, which was the very last thing that Auld Jim Fletcher needed.

He crunched across the piles of broken milk crates and smashed bottles, clenching and unclenching the great big gnarled country hands that could cradle a delicate petal or crush human jaws. 'Whit the fuck wiz that an' which ane o' ye little evil bastards done it?'

Johnny shuffled forward pointing vaguely behind him in the direction of the girders. 'I seen somebody on the bridge drappin' a stane on us, Jim.'

Jim was shaking with rage and advancing on Johnny, his rock-hard fists twitching with desire. 'D'ye think Ah'm a neepheid?' he whispered down at the tarmac. 'D'ye think Ah'm daft enough tae swally some shite aboot somebody on the bridge drappin' a stane? At this time in the moarnin'? Waitin' there half the nicht tae drap a stane, wiz he?' He had looked up from the road surface now and was staring red-eyed at Johnny. 'Who wiz it?' he roared. 'Which ane o' yez wiz it?' Auld Jim glared at each of us in turn till his blazing eyes fell on to the pitiful figure of Wee Good John, who was now openly weeping into the sleeves of his pullover. 'Yoo, ye wee bastard. Tell me whit happened or Ah'll seck the whole lot o' yez.'

Wee John started to own up, even though Jim was homicidal and he knew his confession would cost him his job and several of his front teeth at least. 'I canna let yez tak' this fur me, lads. It wiz—'

Johnny suddenly stepped between Jim and Wee John. 'It wiz a lad on the bridge drapped a stane on us, like Ah telt ye. Did onybody else see him?' He turned to us with a hard authority that I'd never seen on his face before.

Frank was the first to catch on. 'Ah seen somebody movin' on the bridge, Johnny. Ah didnae see the stane, mind, but Ah definitely seen movemint.'

'Ah seen him clear,' says Steevie, who had years of experience giving water-tight statements to the boabies. 'He wiz aboot ten or elivin, wi' a dark jerkin an' dark blue troozers. He leaned ower the railin' an' drapped a stane. Then he legged it ower there.' Steevie's thin, noxious fag drew an unerring line of light brown smoke from right to left along the parapet of the bridge, tracing the perpetrator's escape route. Steevie was so convincing that for a moment I began to doubt that I really had seen Wee Good throwing a golf ball.

Everybody was beginning to look at me and Gordon and Si, and it was obviously our turn to decide whether to be with Captain Bligh in the wee longboat or Fletcher Christian onboard the good ship *Bounty*, so I decided to fling in my hand with the mutineers. My flimsy offering of 'Ah seen a wee laddie jist like Johnny said' wouldn't have made much difference on its own, but once Gordon went on to describe the little culprit as having a bit of a limp and Si added that he was fairly sure he had blue eyes, it was pretty clear that the crew would all stick to the story and Jim would have a hard job getting anybody to deviate from the script, even though everybody standing among the smashed bottles and the shredded tyre knew it was complete bullshit.

'Ah ken whit yez are a' up tae, yez little bastards. Ah ken fine it wiz that wee mongrel that done whitever he done.' Jim's venom flew from the tip of his index finger into Wee John's forehead. 'Ah dinna ken whit ye done, ye wee whelp, but Ah ken ye done it, an' ye'll paiye fur it soon enough, mark ma words. An' you, Johnny' – turning to face his trusted lieutenant, his senior milk laddie – 'ye're jist like the rest o' them now.' Auld Jim Fletcher stood among the wreckage of his milk crates and broken bottles looking tired, angry, frustrated and almost as pitiful as Wee Good John kneeling in the road.

I didn't know what to do or how to try to help them – John having fucked up again and Jim facing a situation that undermined the values that had sustained him throughout his long life. The peasants had stormed the Bastille and neither Auld Jim, Wee John nor I knew what was supposed to happen next. Fortunately, Avril saved me from my part in this dilemma by taking control of the situation like the professional operations manager she was.

'Richt, yez laddies,' she shouted from the step in a clear, calm voice. 'Git a' this shite aff the road, an' git ony whole bottles back in the crates. Si an' Goardin, yez twa git awa' doon tae the bridge an' start scrapin' a' the gless tae the kerb. Wullie an' Steevie, git the brush an' shuvil oot o' the cab an' start clearin' a' this broken gless fae roond the larry. JOHN!' Wee John leaped to his feet. 'Git yer wee arse up here an' start sweepin' the gless aff the deck o' the larry. An' you, Frank, you an' me'll cheenge the tyire.' We all leaped to it like marine commandoes. Then very softly she turned towards her father. 'Mibbie ye should go back intae yer cab, Dad.'

Auld Jim forced his eyes away from the Kingsway and started to plod back to the driver's seat and the dregs of his punctured hip flask. Johnny had been deliberately left out of the rescue plan.

While we were all sweeping, scraping, shovelling and tidying like demons, a little black van mounted the central reservation opposite the truck and a young policeman got out, crisp and full of business. He looked like he was enjoying his fourth week of being a real police constable: you could have cut your thumb on the creases in the sleeves of his uniform, and the peak of his cap was pulled forward till it was level with the bridge of his nose. He strutted slowly across the grass, toecaps gleaming and a neon sign saying, 'I'm in charge,' glowing from his hat. He theatrically pulled an immaculate notebook and pencil from his immaculate breast pocket. Si and Frank started to hum the tune of 'The British Grenadier', Steevie quietly moved his labours to an area that put the lorry between himself and the line of sight of the cop, while Jim stood at the door of his cab and glared at this child in uniform.

As the fresh-faced policeboy and his notebook wandered round the back of the truck, a movement from the wee black van caught my attention and another older, fatter policeman got out and started sauntering towards us.

Avril crunched across the broken glass to stand beside the young cop, while the rest of us continued to make a big show of cleaning up.

'Whit's happened here, then?' said the teenager in the policeman's outfit.

Jim couldn't hold on to his temper any longer. 'Whit d'ye think happened here, ye daft bugger? The larry crashed. That's whit.'

The teenage policeman started to write a literal transcription of what Jim had said in his notebook: 'T-h-e l-a-r-r-y c-r-a-s-h-e-d.'

Jim advanced on him over the top of his crouching milk laddies working hard to restore order to the Kingsway.

Luckily for all of us, the older cop appeared round the side of the truck, nodded towards Avril, and then addressed Auld Jim. 'Ye'll be Jim Fletcher,' he said amiably.

I didn't know if he had a good memory for the people who lived on his beat, or read the name on the truck and put two and two together, or just remembered Jim from previous encounters in the holding cells.

Jim grunted his agreement.

'So, Mr Fletcher, ye've left a bit o' a mess alang the road here. Whit caused ye tae dae this, exacly?'

Auld Jim's moment of decision had come, and we stopped shovelling and scraping so we could see what would happen. Jim flicked his gaze over each of us in turn before he looked Johnny straight in the eyes and said flatly, 'A wee laddie drapped a stane on the larry aff yon bridge.'

'So let me get this right, Mr Fletcher. Whit ye're tellin' me is that at seven fifty-two in the moarnin', a small boy drapped a stane on tae yer mulk larry aff the railway bridge fur nae reason. Is that correct?'

The young policeman carried on writing furiously in his notebook.

'Aye,' said Jim. 'Ah seen him daein' it an' so did a' ma laddies.'

We fairly fell over each other chorusing our agreement.

'Well, Mr Fletcher, sir,' he said, sliding his own notebook deliberately back into his breast pocket. 'That's the biggest load o' haverin' shite Ah've heard in a lang while.' The young cop's knees visibly buckled and his pencil scrawled an involuntary wavy line down the page of his pad. The veteran policeman continued, 'Ah dinna ken whit happened here, an' Ah suppose Ah nivir will, but if a wee laddie an' a stane is yer story, an' you an' a' they laddies are stickin' tae it, then that's whit happened. Ah'll get on tae Interpol right away in case he tries tae flee the country.'

The two policemen strolled around the truck surveying the damage and our attempts to clean up the road. The young guy continued taking copious notes, while the old guy just looked around at nothing in particular.

When they got back to Avril, the older cop said, 'Jist tell yer lads tae forget that an' get the larry back tae the depot. Ye've got work tae dae an' they've tae get tae skael. We'll sort oot the mess.'

But the rookie policeman just had to have his last moment of power. 'Ah noticed that yer front affside tyire's a wee bit baldie,' he said to Auld Jim in his best authoritative voice. 'This may well have been a contribootarry factor tae the larry leavin' the designated vehic'lur area of the carriageway.' He was well chuffed with himself now, so he carried on, 'Ah wid strongly suggest that ye replace this tyire right away if ye dinna want tae git yersel' intae serious trubble.'

Jim's mouth began working involuntarily and his face took on a demonic, twitching life of its own. 'Ye cheeky wee bastard,' he shouted at the startled young cop. 'Ah'll show ye whit serious trubble feels like when Ah gie ye—'

'CONSTABLE GALLOWAY!'

Everybody, even Jim, stopped and whirled round to stare at the fat old sergeant. 'We've done aboot everythin' we can dae here fur the moment. Awa' ye go back tae the van an' get a brush an' shuvil an' twa or three cones tae put on the road.'

Constable Galloway was only too glad to take his older colleague's advice and he marched purposefully towards the wee van on his errand with as much dignity and pride as he could salvage.

'Whit ma faither wiz tryin' tae say tae yer mate there, Sergeant, is that he's made arrangements fur ma brother tae pick up a tyire fae the scrappy's later the day, so there'll be a new tyire on the wheel fur the moarnin's roond. Is that no' richt, Dad?'

Auld Jim just continued to glare maliciously into the back of the retreating young policeman.

'Well, that's jist fine, lass.' The old cop smiled. 'That'll keep a'body happy.' Then he turned to the old, tired proprietor of Fletcher's Dairies and I could only just make out the soft words 'See when yer laddie gets ye a tyire oot the scrapyaird, Jim?'

'Aye?'

'Ask him tae get ye an up-tae-date tax disc while he's there.'

As the old sergeant ambled away to pass on some quiet words of wisdom to Constable Galloway at the rear of the wee van, Jim Fletcher gazed along the Kingsway, back to a time when his mind was clear and his reactions were fast, to a place where whisky only cost twelve and six a bottle and a huge iron fleet of

British battleships ruled the oceans of the world, to a time when milk laddies knew their place and any young smart-arse boaby who spoke to him like that would have been lying on his back unconscious before his 'contribootarry factors' and his helpful suggestions were halfway out of his mouth. Now he looked like an old man who had forgotten where he lived: confused and frustrated at the spectre of his own senility.

Then something astonishing happened. Normally, Johnny walked like a cool cat, looking moodily down at the ground four feet ahead, thumbs in pockets, and slightly rotating either shoulder in a motion counter to the stride of his legs. So when his right foot stepped forward, his hunched left shoulder glided ever so subtly in the direction of where the foot would land, thus (he believed) creating the impression of the movements of a big predatory cat: smouldering, moody and sensual. This time, though, he just walked forward like any ordinary, awkward fifteen-year-old boy and stood almost humbly in front of Auld Jim. Elvis would have been ashamed.

'This huz been a bit o' a bastard fur us a', Jim, eh?'

Auld Jim turned suspiciously to face him, and Avril looked on with equal narrow-eyed concern. 'Aye, so?'

'Weel, Jim, Ah wiz thinkin'. We've a' fell in the shite here, so how do we no' work thegither tae pull oorsel's oot o' the shite? A'thegither, like?'

Avril, the laddies and me had given up being

discreet and were openly staring at the unfolding drama, trying to keep up with all the subtle nuances of tone, inflection and body language.

'Weel, git on wi' it,' said the oak-hard figure beside the cab of his dented milk lorry.

'Whit are ye sayin'?' Johnny swallowed a wee drop of his saliva and a large bit of his pride. 'Hows aboot this, Jim? Hows aboot we a' chip in fae oor tips towards the damage tae the larry an' replacin' the bottles an' that?' He made an inclusive sweeping gesture over all the rest of us behind him.

Jim just stood there, his mind searching for a scam.

Gordon piped up, 'How aboot half a croon a week fae each o' us till it's a' paiyed aff, Jim? That's seventeen an' six a week.'

All of us voiced our agreement. 'That's fair, Goardin.'

'We could manage twa an' six sharely?'

'Coont me in, Johnny.'

Only Steevie, who looked a bit puzzled, and Wee Good John, surveying the scene through wet red eyes, said nothing.

After a short pause, Jim growled back at Johnny, 'Aye, richt, son. That'll dae. Ye see Avril aboot it.' Honour was served and Auld Jim pulled himself into his cab, toasted his victory with the remnants of his hip flask, and started the engine.

Avril threw the shredded tyre on to the back of the lorry and off we went.

Fletcher's Dairies had insurance that covered for just such an eventuality and I've no doubt that Avril doubled the number of bottles and crates lost. Legitimate quotations were obtained for work on the truck from two of Jim's dodgy mates and were agreed by the insurance company before two signed blank invoices materialised and one of Auld Jim's panel-beater mates went to work in the milk shed at the depot. After a bit of a respray paint job one Sunday by a lad on our round from whom we stopped collecting milk money for a while, we were back as good as new.

Avril collected the two and six from each of us for four weeks. On the fifth week, as she was dishing out the wages, she whispered, 'Ah'll no' be takin' ony mair, lads, but Ah'll tell ma dad ye're a' still paiyin' up. Wheesht now.'

I don't know how long she kept it going, but I'm sure that Auld Jim Fletcher thought he had netted about fifty pounds in profit from the whole episode.

'Serves the wee bastards richt.'

Chapter Thirteen

A Common Water Carrier

The Shoshone describe a boy's journey into manhood
as leaving the place of the 'common water carrier'
and entering the place of the 'warrior'. I was leaving
the place of the 'common milk carrier' to enter
God knew where.

Avril and Si were deep in quiet conversation at the
front of the truck. We carried on loading up the crates,
watching out of the corner of our eyes as she listened
and occasionally nodded at what Si was saying. Finally,
she smiled, rubbed his shoulder, and said something
we couldn't hear.

'Somethin's wrang wi' Si, Wullie,' Steevie said gravely. 'Look, Avril's rubbin' his shoolder.'

I tried to be as gentle as I could. 'He's tellin' her he's jackin', mate.'

Steevie blinked back at me in disbelief. 'How wid Si gie up the mulk when he's makin' a Klon? His ma needs the money, a'body kens that. Si widnae quit that easy – he's nae quitter, no' Si.' Steevie looked at me defiantly, daring me to contradict him as the thought of losing his soulmate began to sink in.

Steevie was still staring at me when Avril strode purposefully round to the back of the lorry with her arm round Si. We knew that a serious announcement was imminent. We left the rest of the crates on the ground or half stacked on the lorry and stood waiting for the news that would be no surprise to anyone except Steevie.

Si cleared his throat and said, 'Ah'm leavin', lads. Ah've jist gae in ma twa weeks' notice tae Avril.'

Steevie sat on the flatbed of the lorry with his legs dangling over the huddin' rail. 'How, Si? How are ye leavin'? It's good here. We mak' a forchin an' ye can gie loads o' money tae yer mum. Hiv ye got a full-time joab or somethin'?' Steevie's voice quivered with disappointment and frustration, and I realised just how deeply he felt for his friend.

'Nae, Steevie, Ah've no' got a joab. Ah've been speakin' tae Mitchell, the head o' science, an' he said he thinks Ah could get intae ane o' them Inglish universities, like Oxfurd or that. He said he thinks Ah could get a skollurship an' a bursery, but Ah wid hae tae jack in the mulk so Ah could spend a' ma time studyin'. Ah wid need tap marks in ma O levels an' Highers if Ah wanted tae get a bursery an' get in, ye see. Ah've spoke tae ma muthir an' she says Ah've tae grab this wi' baith hands.'

'Yer muthir's right, Si,' said Gordon.

'If ye want tae go tae Oxfurd, they'll ask ye things. They only let snobs an' rich fowk in.' Frank took on the role of the grand inquisitor, giving a very bad impersonation of an upper-class English accent. 'Now, Russell, dear boy, we have strict tests to see who we're going to let in our university.'

'OK,' says Si, 'go ahead.'

Frank made a big play of looking at pretend notes and at last asked, 'How many rooms do you think are in the average council house?'

Si was way ahead and happy to play the game, replying in an equally unconvincing Home Counties accent, 'Well, not including the drawing room, billiards room, conservatory and the below-stairs servants' quarters, I'd say about twelve.'

'That's our kind of fellow,' whooped Frank. 'Obviously never had any dealings with the working class. Welcome to the university, old bean. By the way, you wouldn't happen to have any sort of qualifications or such, would you? Doesn't really matter of course, but we have to ask nowadays.'

But Gordon wasn't going to give him a scholarship to Oxford as easily as that. 'One question,' he says. 'Tell us a bit about your family, particularly your father. Was he in the Guards, or was he a naval chap?'

Si was as sharp as usual. 'Well, Father resigned his commission in the Life Guards to become a coalman. Then after a couple of months delivering coal, he fucked off and left me, Mummy and my wee sister to fend for ourselves. So Mummy sold off the family estates in Norfolk and took up a position slicing bacon in the Co-op.'

Gordon nodded appreciatively, but played the dean of the faculty to the hilt. 'What about your school, though, Russell?' he said with mock gravitas. 'It really matters to us where a boy was educated. Tell us, Russell, was it Rugby you went to?'

Steevie was totally bewildered, but tried to make some contribution with 'Rugby's that gemme the toffs play wi' a bent ba', aye?'

Si nodded at Steevie. 'That's right, mate, but it's the name o' a school in England as well.'

Steevie was now even more confused. 'Imagine onybody ca'in' a skael efter a gemme. That's like goin' tae a skael ca'd "fitba'" or "dominoes". They're totally daft them Inglish.'

Si completely ignored him and turned back to the

dean of the faculty. 'No, it was actually Kirkton High I attended.'

The whole interview panel drew back from the huddin' rail in admiration.

'Kirkton, eh? A fine school with a noble tradition dating back nearly three whole years,' Frank announced.

'Splendid,' said Johnny. 'Ticketty fucking boo, old boy – you're in. We'll have you rowing up the Thames in no time.'

Si's leaving pushed wedges into the little hairline cracks in my perfect wealthy world. I began to notice that my other schoolmates were going out to the ice rink on Saturday nights when I was getting ready for bed, and groups of lads were starting to hang about with groups of girls while I was trotting around pre-fabs collecting milk money. Lolling sexily against the huddin' rail on the morning returns to the depot didn't inspire nearly as much awe as it used to, and looking at the faces of my schoolmates chatting on the pavements, I realised that the usual expressions of respect and wide-eyed adoration were imperceptibly turning into mild disinterest. Worse still, the only ones gazing admiringly seemed to be twelve-year-old kids. It just wasn't cool being a milk laddie any more.

It also became obvious that working milk boys were getting left behind at school. Kids in the 'A' classes were starting to talk openly about O levels and unashamedly studying to try to pass exams, and even the playground talk of the 'B' stream was interspersed with references to 'Skael Laivin' Sirtificits' and 'Whit subjicts are ye goin' fur?'

Little by little the haze I'd been living in began to clear. Daylight filtered through, evaporating the mist, until I saw what I'd suspected for ages: my mum had been right all along. That boring stuff about O levels and my 'feutchir' that she'd been nipping my head with for the past twelve months really did matter, and I'd been too wealthy and preoccupied to notice. The day when the awful truth at last stared straight into my face, I got the shock of my life. We were in a history class and, as usual, Gordon and me had dozed off. You could tell who was on the milk because they were either asleep in class or hadn't handed in any homework. Suddenly, we heard 'McKINLAY!' I snapped awake and looked over at Gordon. He was sitting bolt upright, trying to appear alert and failing, while I frantically attempted to marshal my senses in case it was me next.

Mr Watson imperiously stared at Gordon. 'You've no doubt been listening to our discussions, McKinlay, so can you please give us your views on the effect of the repeal of the Corn Laws on English agrarian society?'

I knew that Gordon was still mentally in bed or running his milk round. I also knew that, like me, he didn't know what Corn Laws were, and didn't realise they'd been introduced in the first place, never mind repealed. My poor half-asleep best friend began to mumble some drivel about Tolpuddle martyrs and Spinning Jennies. It was increasingly clear that he hadn't got a clue about corn, or laws, or history, or bugger all else that we needed to know. He was going to fail his O-level history and so was I. Worse, he was going to fail his O-level everything and so was I.

This wasn't a joke or a game any more. Gordon and me had swaggered so far down the wide highway leading to 'No Qualifications at All' that I could visualise myself as a twenty-six-year-old milk boy with no qualifications and even fewer prospects. The thought didn't charm me one bit.

'Come out here, McKinlay!' Gordon shuffled out to the front of the class. 'I sometimes think I'm wasting my time trying to teach you anything, McKinlay.' Gordon looked down at the teacher's knees. 'I don't mind wasting my time on the likes of you – that's part of being a teacher here – but what I won't tolerate is disrespect. Falling asleep when I'm talking is the height of bad manners, and so you need to be taught some manners, don't you, McKinlay?'

Gordon looked up into Mr Watson's eyes and said, 'I don't know, sir.'

'Well, you soon will know, laddie. Get your hands out.' He reached into the drawer of his desk and took out the leather belt that he relied on to maintain the discipline and respect of children. The belt was about eighteen inches long and half an inch thick, with a shaped part to hold at one end and three leather thongs at the business end.

Gordon held his hands straight out in front of him so that Mr Watson could deliver a blow like a fast bowler going for the middle stump. Whack! The sound of the belt hitting his palms made everybody grimace. Gordon instinctively pulled his stinging hands behind his back.

'Again, McKinlay,' said Mr Watson.

Gordon once more held out his hands. The thwack of leather on Gordon's red palms gave everybody a bad taste in their mouth. There was no need for this.

'Sit down, McKinlay. Now, let that be a lesson to all of you who haven't learned any respect.' Watson smirked, flexing the leather belt between his hands, then returning it to the drawer.

I looked over at my mate, biting his lip and holding back pain, and back at Mr Watson. Suddenly, I thought, Ye dinna deserve tae get away wi' this, ye bullyin' bastard. Before I realised what I was doing, I'd said, 'Sorry, sir, could ye say a' that again, please? Ah didnae catch whit ye said there. Ah wiz dozin' aff, ye see.'

A few moments later, out in front of the class, the pain shot up my arms as Mr Watson's respect-enforcer hit my outstretched palms. Somehow, though, it almost felt like he was doing me a service: drawing a line under my days of delivering milk, falling asleep in class and not seeing anything beyond my tips and Avril's pay packet. For fifteen months I'd basked in the glow of fame and fortune, but now I was starting to get tired: tired of getting up in the middle of the night, tired of being cold and wet, tired of being exploited, just tired of the whole game. The truth was, I had huddin'-rail combat fatigue. Standing there, with my arms outstretched, palms facing up, as the leather belt hit my hands again, my eyes filled with tears.

Mr Watson saw the tears and thought that he'd won. He'd exposed a little arrogant smart-arse in front of his class and could afford to be magnanimous. 'Go and sit down now, Robertson. I think you've learned your lesson.' His voice was almost kind.

I'd felt much harder belts than Watson's, belts that really did bring you to the verge of sobbing pain, but I'd never known corporal punishment to have such an effect on me. Tomorrow, I would tell Avril I was leaving.

Early the next morning, I took a deep breath and walked towards Avril, who was stacking full crates on the back of the lorry in the freezing pre-dawn. I wasn't six feet from her when Johnny pushed in front of me and announced to the world, 'Ah'm packin' in, Avril.' The words were delivered in a cloud of vapour as his warm breath hit the icy air. 'Ah've got enough fur ma bike now. Ah telt yez that Ah wid only work on the mulk till Ah hud enough fur ma bike,' he said almost apologetically. He was more worried about maintaining his image in front of us than he was with tendering his resignation.

Everybody knew that he'd never get a motorbike. The truth was that he was becoming concerned that being a milk laddie was bad for his image, and he thought he'd better move before he turned from a milk boy into a milkman.

I didn't have the heart just then to tell Avril that I was leaving too, so I waited it out a little longer. Meanwhile, Johnny trained his replacement. It made me smile watching him bragging to this wee boy about the various women on the round who fancied him. 'See her on the second tap richt? Ye want tae see her giein' me the mulk money. Strokes ma hand when she puts the money in it she diz.' His semi got even more special attention through his pocket as he bade farewell to all the women on his round he was abandoning. Finally, two weeks later, Johnny and his best friend Semi rode off into the sunset together, legends in their own lifetime, to take up their positions as two tiny wee fish in a vast ocean.

Johnny's replacement was called Larry – short for Lorenzo Giuseppe Isabella. As soon as we knew his full name, we had him clocked: 'Diz yer dad hae the ice-creamer at the tap o' Portree Avenue, Larry?'

This shop, the Neapolitan Ice-Cream Parlour, was about five hundred yards from the gates of our school, and every lunchtime hordes of kids jostled and pushed their way into the wee premises to get their daily fix.

Three generations of Larry Giuseppe Isabellas worked in the shop. Larry's dad and granddad laboured there from dawn till dusk, seven days a week, and young Larry did his bit by adding his little muscle power on Saturday afternoons stacking shelves and moving boxes. Larry's dad was in charge of the real products, like boxes of Cadbury's Roses and twenty-packs of Benson & Hedges, while Granddad Larry's department was more specialised, having only one product line.

'Whit hae ye got fur thruppence, Larry?'

'Highland-a-Toffee,' the Italian replied.

'OK, gie me three Highland-a-Toffees.'

Three Woodbine cigarettes would dutifully appear on the counter.

The game made all the wee schoolkids feel grown-up and in-the-know, like the guy who had been told to whisper, 'Joe sent me,' through the grille of the Chicago speakeasy.

Everybody knew that Granddad Larry was sharp as a tack, and a very wealthy man, having made a separate small fortune independently of the shop trade. This made Steevie suspicious of young Lorenzo Giuseppe Isabella's motives for wanting to become a milk laddie:

why would anybody from a wealthy shop-owning dynasty want to work on the milk?

'How huv ye got tae work on the mulk, Larry? A'body kens that yer granddad's minted.'

It was at times like these that I appreciated the true value of all the decorum and etiquette classes that Steevie must have attended during his time at the exclusive finishing school in Switzerland. Surely a glittering career in Her Majesty's diplomatic service awaited the future Sir Steven.

'It's ma ain wee statement, like. It's tae show that Ah could mak' ma ain way withoot haein' tae work fur ma granddad in his bloody shop. Ah could earn money without him, ye ken.'

Larry was clearly railing against some demons, so Steevie unselfishly stepped forward to help. 'Ah'll gie ye a hand wi' makin' yer statement there, Larry. How aboot Ah'll gie ye a half-croon fur every twa ounces o' Virginia Flake that ye can pochul oot the shop an' we'll go halfies on the profit fae the sales an' a'? That wid stick it tae yer granddad good an' proper, aye?'

Lorenzo declined Steevie's kind offer.

I waited a full two weeks before I even thought about telling Avril I was leaving, then another week just to make sure that Larry had his round reasonably well memorised. I told her when she gave me my pay packet after collecting the milk money on Friday night.

'Ah'm leavin', Avril,' was all I could muster.

'Ah ken that, Wullie. Ah've kent that fur three weeks now. An' three weeks behind ye will be yer mate Goardin.' Avril had learned a lot about people after employing adolescents all these years.

Having worked with her almost every day for the last fifteen months, I felt I'd let her down somehow and had to say something. 'Ah'll no' let ye doon, though, ye dinna need tae worry. Ah'll train ma replacement real good.'

'Aye, Wullie, Ah ken that fine. Ye're a good wee laddie an' ye've been a good wee worker.' Avril gently pinched my cheek. 'Ye can bugger aff now an' git they crates up on the larry.'

So I trained my wee apprentice, whose name I can't even remember, the best I possibly could. I showed him the round and I tried to pass on everything Avril had taught me and everything I'd picked up along the way. I even toyed with the idea of telling him that Johnny had shagged three of the women customers on the round and Wee Good John had thrown a golf ball over the Kingsway Bridge and caught it at the other side, but I resisted the temptation.

Avril was right: three weeks later, Gordon jacked in as well.

Gordon and me didn't exactly distinguish ourselves in the 'gaining-O-levels' department, but it wasn't the total disaster it would have been if we'd stayed on the milk for the final six or seven months before the exams. We managed to scrape four or five certificates each, which just about kept my mum off my back and allowed us both to apply for half-a-dozen reasonable jobs. I had achieved a real mix-and-match of certificates in totally unrelated subjects, like art and mathematics, so I had no idea what I was going to do with my new qualifications. Even I realised that there couldn't be many potential employers out there who would want to take on such a well-rounded individual as me. After all, how many companies desperately needed somebody to provide them with watercolour paintings of quadratic equations?

Most of us were pretty much in the same boat. Everybody except Wee Good John left the milk during the last nine months to make our own way in the big world outside the protection of the pack. The humour and camaraderie of the lorry had bound us together for nearly a year and a half, but now we were all just individual young laddies wondering what was going to happen next.

So what did happen next? What became of the crew of the good ship *Mulk Larry*? What became of the tightly knit team who had laughed, cried, blasphemed, stuck together, fell over and sung Beatles songs while clinging on to the huddin' rail for so many miles? Well, I'll tell you about the fate of each of us as best I know.

Johnny: nobody really knows what happened to Johnny Bonnar; he just sort of disappeared. A couple of lads said they heard he bought a Triumph Tiger motorbike and he and his semi headed to London to front up a rock band. He probably did head for somewhere like London, or Amsterdam, or Marrakesh, but on a bus, and I think he most likely ended up as an estate agent or a porn star. Johnny and all his ilk slowly faded into the distance, combing their greasy Brylcreemed hair and polishing their winklepickers.

Wee Good: despite the incident at the bridge, John stayed on the milk for ages. Eventually, he quit and got a job as a clerk in the wages department of one of the biggest jute mills in Dundee. The company had been trading for over a century and a half, and had more than two thousand employees and massive order books. Within ten years of Wee Good's arrival, however, the entire Dundee jute trade collapsed, propelling the city into two decades of the most significant economic and social depression in its history.

Steevie: Steevie didn't manage to obtain any certificates at all as a result of his three partial years of state education, and he didn't give a shit. His dad got him a job on the building site as an apprentice plasterer's labourer, with a view to eventually working his way up to an apprentice plasterer if he showed promise. There was no way Steevie would want to become a plasterer: it was too much hard work. Anyway, he would make much more money than a tradesman through running sweepstakes, organising cash-only weekend jobs – 'homers' – and pilfering cuttings of copper pipe off the site. After less than eighteen months, though, he was invited to join the official pub darts team at the Silver Birch, the youngest person ever to have gained such a singular honour.

Si: Oxford University couldn't wait to get their hands on Russell Malcolm, and offered him scholarships, bursaries, subsidies in this, that and the other, and free lemonade for life if he would only come to them instead of the other lot. Si graciously accepted, and read things like pure mathematics, quantum mechanics and 'hard workie oots' for the next several years, until he gained his doctorate in 'incomprehensible studies' and went on to become one of the country's leading authorities in something that only he and twelve other people in the world understood. Last I heard, his mum had abandoned her vocation as a bacon-slicer in Kirkton and was living with Si's wee sister in a comfortable bungalow in the posher part of Broughty Ferry in the suburbs of Dundee.

Fat Boab: Robert Findlay had all the qualities that the senior executives of Dundee Corporation needed in an employee at that time. He was white, Protestant, a stalwart member of the Church and a corporal in the

Boys' Brigade. Even better, his father was a captain in the same Boys' Brigade unit, an elder of the Church of Scotland, a long-serving member of his local Orange Order, and regularly shared a small whisky or two with a few of the town councillors who were members of his local Masonic Lodge. So it didn't come as a big shock when Boab started work in the office of the roads department of the 'cooncil'. When his employers discovered that he had three O levels and his mum made shortbread, his place within the higher echelons of the cooncil was assured. 'This laddie will be Lord Provist one day, mark ma words.'

Goardin: my friend Gordon had been searching for an authority figure since before I met him. His poor wee grannie couldn't provide the rulebook he so badly needed, nor could any of our teachers or even Avril. I really think the nearest he got was when he was with my mum, but she already had three sons and didn't have the time or the inclination to become surrogate mother to a fourth. Given no boundaries, Gordon became a complete 'sky's the limit' person who thought that controls and rules and restrictions were for everybody else, and that *he* was capable of anything. So when he saw an advert for a trainee executive in the local paper, Gordon knew this job was tailor-made for him because he could do anything he wanted and it was his destiny to become an executive. Nobody had ever told him otherwise. So he applied for the post and was duly appointed trainee executive at the huge linoleum factory on the outskirts of the city.

'Whit dae ye akchully dae, Goardin?' I inquired, as you would.

'Well, mainly Ah stack pallits an' unload the larries wi' the kemiculs an' that.'

I wasn't at all impressed. 'That's no' whit exekitives dae. Exekitives sit in offices an' drink coffee while ithir fowk dae a' the work.'

Gordon smiled like a loving father responding to a child's naïve questions about God. 'Ye dinna understand, Wullie,' he soothed. 'An exekitive huz got tae understand the business fae the bottom up. How could Ah mak' major exekitive disishuns aboot the feutchir o' the company unless Ah ken whit's happenin' at the sharp end?'

I couldn't hold it back. 'They're takin' a len o' ye, Goardin. Ye're no' an exekitive; ye're a labourer. Tell the boy tae go piss up a rope an' get anithir joab wi' some kind o' real prospects. Ye're sharp an' quick an' good wi' people, an' ye can write stuff better than ony o' us. Ye could be a skael teacher, or even a lekchirur at a college. Ye dinna see many lekchirurs humpin' pallits aroond.'

Gordon looked at me like he never had before, a look that told me I had no right to talk to him like that, and that he was hurt that I had. I didn't know it at the time, but this was the first tiny movement in the drifting apart of me and the closest friend I'd ever had. The irony is that Gordon now writes 'stuff' for several universities and 'lekchires' all over the UK.

Me: it turned out that somebody actually did want a mathematical painter after all. Unbeknown to me, being not bad at drawing and mathematics was just the combination of talents needed to become an apprentice architectural draughtsman, and a local building company happened to be looking for just such a person. Luckily, Leonardo da Vinci must have been working on a painting of some woman or other on that Friday and missed seeing the advert in the paper, because I got a letter right away inviting me for an interview in response to my application.

My wee grannie was very fond of giving me advice in the form of little sayings and phrases that I suppose her mother had taught her as a child. My great-grannie must have thought this was about the only legacy she could pass on that had any value, but most of the time I just smiled and agreed without having any notion what she was on about, like when she told me that she was glad I hadn't started smoking yet. 'Ye're best tae bide aff the fags as lang as ye can, Wullie,' she said, lighting up her Embassy. 'They can gie ye broonkaitis.' She must have thought this was the same condition as nicotine-stained 'broon fingers', except on your 'kaitis'.

In her more lucid moments she could come out with

a short, simple statement that hit the nail on the head and summed up both the problem and its solution. When we had just moved to the new estate and a big laddie in the street was throwing his weight around and terrifying all the wee lads, including me, she said, smiling, 'Wullie, mind this – it's no' the size o' the dog in the fight. It's the size o' the fight in the dog.' With this in my mind, the big bully turned out to be a marshmallow, as they usually do.

When my mum was still doing my head about being on the milk and missing my sleep, my grannie had given me really valuable advice that I hadn't appreciated till it was almost too late. 'Ye're a smert laddie, Wullie. Dinna be like the rest o' them. Get yersel' an educashun an' the heaviest things ye'll hae tae lift is a pencil an' yer fat paiye packet.'

When I was miraculously offered a job as an apprentice architectural draughtsman after the interview, I thought, Well, at least half my grannie's advice was correct. The heaviest things that architectural draughtsmen lift are pencils, right enough.

Unfortunately, the second half of her prediction wasn't quite as accurate, because the 'paiye packet' of a first-year apprentice draughtsman weighed about the same as the pencil. As a milk laddie, I came home with about two pounds and two shillings (tax-free) in my pocket every week. When I graduated to the dizzy heights of apprentice architectural draughtsman, working forty hours a week, fifteen pounds and eight shillings (less tax) were paid into my new bank account every month. But it wasn't about the money; I had a 'feutchir'.

Every morning just before eight o'clock, I stood at the bus-stop on the main road through our housing estate waiting for the bus that would take me to work. Minutes before the bus arrived, the Fletcher's Dairies milk lorry would come roaring past with empty milk bottles rattling in the crates and seven wee laddies hanging off the back. For the first few months I was still waking at half past four in the morning, and Avril still recognised me at the bus-stop and waved, but gradually I occasionally slept till seven and Avril occasionally missed a wave. Eventually, I was sleeping until seven every morning and Avril wasn't acknowledging me at all.

The thing that really got me, though, was the milk laddies. They all looked as if they belonged in primary school as they lolled on the back step looking relaxed and cool, laughing and posing. I could see a diminutive Johnny lookalike thrusting his pelvis forward as he stood on the step grasping the huddin' rail behind his back, and I even thought I spotted the poor soul who had inherited Wee Good John's crown. The one I recognised instantly was me: the little boy looking so grown-up doing real man's work and probably ending up with more disposable income than his dad. The same boy who only four years before had been galloping around on an imaginary white stallion with a plastic belt and holster hanging from the waist of his grey flannel shorts, firing caps from a shiny metal six-gun at 'no good varmints' wearing red bandanas and National Health specs.

Thanks to Auld Jim and Avril Fletcher, I had experienced riches that I wouldn't know again for a very long time. The heels of our expensive Beatle boots clicked along the pavement when me and Gordon graced the city-centre streets, and I owned a top-of-the-range record player and every record the Beatles had made.

Because of my mum's foresight and my grannie's daft little pearls of wisdom, I had nine pounds and fifteen shillings in a bank account for my 'feutchir' and the much more valuable prospect of a real career as an architectural draughtsman.

And thanks to Gordon and the rest of my shipmates, July 1962 to October 1963 would be a time in my life I would never forget.

Postscript

I managed to track down Avril, and met with her in November 2008. She's lived on her own in a lovely wee flat in the west end of the city since Sabre and Double Ecks died in quick succession. She's still unbelievably full of energy and inspiringly active, and can remember every single customer delivery on every laddie's section of the whole round. Best of all, she looks as if she could still beat me and the rest of the crew through a morning's delivery if she had to.

When I phoned to ask if I could come and see her, I was all set to give a lengthy explanation of who I was, which years I'd worked for her and even who some of the other crew were, in case they might have left a bigger impression than me. Her reply nearly made me drop the phone, because as soon as I told her my name and said that I used to be one of her laddies, she remembered me instantly. Without prompting, she even asked if I was still friends with Gordon.

Meeting Avril after so long was quite an experience for me. I was truly amazed that she could clearly remember so many boys who had worked for her more than forty-five years ago. After all, she must have had several score of wee laddies running the delivery rounds in her time. It was even more astonishing when she told me that she had no regrets about devoting her life to the family business and its physically and mentally punishing duties, especially when she confided that she had known all along that it was in terminal decline. Ordinary punters were able to buy fridges and cars, so why would they need to rely on milk laddies supplying their doorstep every day? At the time, though, we all thought that Avril was, well, timeless. We saw her inspiring her crew of laddies to run themselves ragged for her for ever. A kind of milk-lorry *Flying Dutchman*.

The revelation that touched me most, though, was when she admitted to 'Feelin' hert sorry fur ma laddies sometimes, runnin' through the rain an' sleet an' sna' an' slippin' aboot on icy pavements every moarnin' fur a pittance. But Ah couldnae let on, ye see.' She poured us each a cup of tea.

'Ye really shouldnae feel like that, Avril,' I said. 'The

way we remember it, we had a ba' an' we made a forchin.'

I poured milk into my tea and offered the jug to Avril.

'Och, no, thanks, Wullie,' she said. 'Ah dinna touch the stuff.'